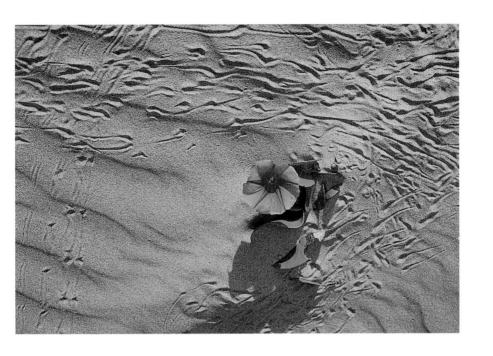

Wildflowers
and Other
Plants
of Texas
Beaches
and Islands

Gorgas Science Foundation, Inc.
Treasures of Nature Series

The Treasures of Nature Series is produced by Gorgas Science Foundation, Inc. (GSF), and reflects its continuing commitment to the production of educational films, books, field guides, and laboratory manuals.

Gorgas Science Foundation, Inc.   80 Fort Brown   Brownsville, Texas 78520

Wildflowers and Other Plants of Texas Beaches and Islands

Alfred Richardson

University of Texas Press, Austin

First edition, 2002

Requests for permission to reproduce material from this work
should be sent to Permissions, University of Texas Press, Box
7819, Austin, TX 78713-7819.

(∞) The paper used in this book meets the minimum
requirements of ANSI/NISO Z39.48-1992 (R1997)
(Permanence of Paper).

Library of Congress Cataloging-in-Publication Data

Richardson, Alfred, 1930–
Wildflowers and other plants of Texas beaches and islands /
Alfred Thomas Richardson.
    p.   cm. — (Treasures of nature series)
Includes bibliographical references (p.   ).
ISBN 0-292-77115-0 (hardcover) — ISBN 0-292-77116-9 (pbk.)
1. Seashore plants—Texas—Identification. 2. Seashore
plants—Texas—Pictorial works. I. Title. II. Series.
QK188 .R533 2002
581.7'699'09764—dc21

2001003891

THIS BOOK IS DEDICATED TO KATIE DEEN.

Captions for front matter images:

Page i: Brazos Island. Railroad Vine (*Ipomoea pes-caprae*) growing at an intersection of sand-crab trails.

Page ii: Mouth of the Rio Grande. A favorite fishing spot on both sides of the river. Camphor Weed (*Heterotheca subaxillaris*) in foreground.

Page ii: Aransas National Wildlife Refuge. Live Oaks. Matagorda Island is barely visible on the horizon.

Page iii: Boca Chica Beach. The Gulf of Mexico on a calm day. While the beach in front of the dunes is mostly bare, the vegetation behind the dunes is often dense.

Page iii: Mustang Island. Dunes near the open beach. Camphor Weed (*Heterotheca subaxillaris*) and Sea Oats (*Uniola paniculata*), with Beach Morning Glory (*Ipomoea imperati*) crisscrossing in the sand.

Page iv: Boca Chica Beach. Sea Oats (*Uniola paniculata*), Camphor Weed (*Heterotheca subaxillaris*), and Beach Tea (*Croton punctatus*).

Page vii: Bolivar Peninsula. Indian Blanket (*Gaillardia pulchella*), Prickly Pear (*Opuntia engelmannii*), and Gaura (*Gaura villosa*) growing within twenty feet of East Bay.

Page xxiii: Padre Island. A hurricane in the Gulf narrowly missed this beach, but still caused enough turbulence to rearrange these dunes, leaving a lot of bare sand. Seaside Goldenrod (*Solidago sempervirens*), Beach Morning Glory (*Ipomoea imperati*), and grasses.

Contents

Acknowledgments

This book was made possible by the help and encouragement of a number of people. Katie and Irv Deen were outstanding in their encouragement and in providing transportation and companionship throughout a large portion of the Texas coast. I am indebted to Scooter Cheatham, author of *The Useful Wild Plants of Texas, the Southeastern and Southwestern United States, the Southern Plains, and Northern Mexico*, for the generous loan of slides of *Cocculus carolinus, Corydalis micrantha, Drosera annua*, and *Tribulus terrestris*. Several plants were photographed, with permission, at the Lady Bird Johnson Wildflower Center in Austin. Professor Billie Turner of the University of Texas at Austin originally suggested this project to me and also identified and gave useful information concerning some of the plants. Tom Robinson provided assistance and companionship on a large number of field trips along the coast. Fred and Marie Webster were generous in sharing information and in giving their time. Dr. Robert Lonard of the University of Texas Pan American identified several of the grasses. Dr. Tom Wendt and David Riskind reviewed the manuscript and provided valuable comments and suggestions. My colleagues Rodney Sullivan and Norman Richard gave many useful suggestions. Alfredo Muñoz provided transportation to beaches difficult to access. William Bishel and the other personnel at the University of Texas Press have been extremely helpful and supportive.

Finally, publication of this book was sponsored by Gorgas Science Foundation.

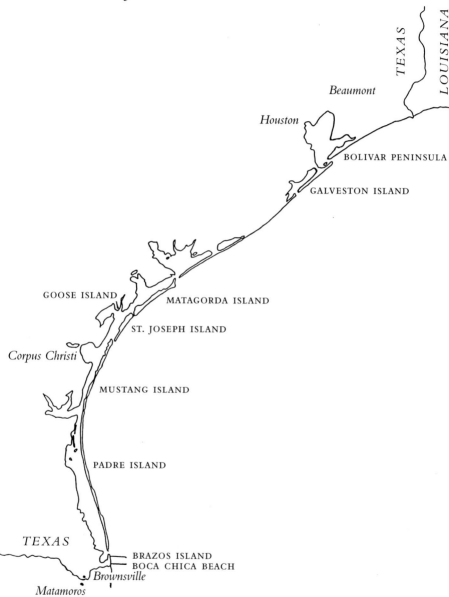

The Texas Gulf Coast

Beaumont

Houston

BOLIVAR PENINSULA

GALVESTON ISLAND

GOOSE ISLAND

MATAGORDA ISLAND

ST. JOSEPH ISLAND

Corpus Christi

MUSTANG ISLAND

PADRE ISLAND

TEXAS

BRAZOS ISLAND
BOCA CHICA BEACH
Brownsville
Matamoros

MEXICO

TEXAS

LOUISIANA

Introduction

The Texas Gulf coast is almost continuously fringed by barrier islands and peninsulas, creating many miles of beaches. The barrier islands are long and narrow and run parallel to the coast. Some of them are true islands; others are connected to the mainland at one end, and are more properly but infrequently called spits. Exceptions are Bolivar Peninsula, near the Louisiana border, and Matagorda Peninsula. Although this book will be useful throughout the Texas coast, the "islands" and beaches specifically dealt with are Bolivar Peninsula, Galveston Island, Matagorda Island, Goose Island, Mustang Island, Padre Island, Brazos Island, and Boca Chica Beach. Of the islands mentioned, Matagorda Island is the widest. Padre Island is the longest barrier island in the world (Britton & Morton 1989).

The local name of Boca Chica Beach includes all the beach area from the Brazos Santiago Pass (now the Brownsville Ship Channel) to the Rio Grande. I have chosen to use the established name of Brazos Island for the northern section (Brazos Santiago Pass to the Boca Chica inlet), and to limit the term "Boca Chica Beach" to the southern section, which extends from Brazos Island to the Rio Grande. Highway 4 makes a convenient dividing line between the two beaches, since it is only a few hundred feet south of the Boca Chica channel.

Most visitors to the beaches, and even many residents, see only the sands between the surf and the first low dunes. Since only a few plants grow in this small section, it is easy to get the impression that these areas consist mostly of barren sand. In fact, the opposite is true. Beyond that first low dune there is an amazing variety and abundance of native plant species. Many of them, like the Indian Blanket, Goldenrod, and Seaside Gerardia, produce great splashes of color. Others produce more modest flowers, or are interesting for their growth habits. Over seven hundred species of flowering plants have been found growing on Texas beaches and islands.

The dunes run parallel with the Gulf shore. Sometimes there are two groups of dunes, resembling a miniature mountain chain, with a valley in between them. Some of the dunes have been known to reach almost forty feet in height (Britton & Morton 1989). The "valley" is higher than the beach area and the salt flats, which are located behind the dunes. Behind the second group of dunes, the terrain gradually slopes down toward the bay, which separates the island from the mainland. This downward slope is interrupted by a number of low, rounded dunes.

There are contrasting areas in which there are no dunes at all. Here the terrain is almost flat from Gulf shore to bay shore. These broad areas may be natural relief zones for the flow of water into and out of the bay during strong storms.

There are various intermediate conditions between the two described extremes. For example, there may be one set of dunes instead of two, or there may be scattered low dunes. A strong hurricane can level many or all of the dunes. Then a gradual rebuilding of the dunes begins.

Generally, the dunes and dune systems contain almost pure sand, and the lower elevations contain varying amounts of clay mixed with the sand. Because of the proximity to the Gulf of Mexico and its bays, there is usually a high saline content. The broadest islands would tend to have some soils with lower salinity and also with more clay and organic content. Also, the grains of sand tend to become larger as one progresses from north to south (Britton & Morton 1989).

The differences in elevation, soil types, and moisture are some of the factors creating many habitats where an amazing number of plant species thrive (Sullivan & Richardson, in manuscript). I have observed that sometimes an elevation change of even one or two inches seems to favor the growth of one species over another. From Aransas Pass northward there is more rainfall (Britton & Morton 1989), and so some plants that grow in the northern portions do not survive farther south.

The intent of this book is to illustrate samples of the flamboyant and more commonly seen, the more modest, and even some of the very tiny but very interesting flowers of the native plants that can be found on our beaches and islands. Plants of the sandy soils are emphasized, but many plants of the heavier soils are also included. About 38 percent of the species reported for the islands are illustrated. It is my hope that, through use of the illustrations and descriptions, the reader will come to appreciate and learn more about the natural flora of this rich area.

Distribution of the plant is noted in each species description. Information on distribution was derived from personal surveys as well as published checklists, which are listed in the bibliography. Since most surveys were done during a single season, there would naturally be some omissions. Therefore, a plant may be listed as growing on just one island, but it could, in fact, be more widespread. In fact, many of the plants illustrated here probably occur throughout our beaches. Many are also found growing on the mainland along or near the bays.

In a technical book, plants would be arranged according to relationships by family, genus, and species. The species is the basic unit. Related species are placed in a group called a genus. Related genera are placed in a group called a family. In this book, the plant families are arranged according to relationships and similarities. Within each family, the genera are arranged in alphabetical order, and within each genus the species are also in alphabetical order.

Common names were derived from the *Manual of the Vascular Plants of Texas* (Correll & Johnston 1970), *Flora of the Texas Coastal Bend* (Jones 1975), *Guide to Grasses of the Lower Rio Grande Valley, Texas* (Lonard 1993), *Plants of the Rio Grande Delta* (Richardson 1995), and the checklists of Padre Island (Lonard et al. 1978, Negrete et al. 1999), Mustang Island (Gillespie 1976), Matagorda Island (Hartman & Smith 1973), Galveston Island State Park, Goose Island State Recreation Area, and Mustang Island State Park (Texas Parks and Wildlife, unpublished).

Recently, several authors have attempted to bring the taxonomy of Texas plants up to date (that is, to establish the single correct name for each plant). One recent book (1997) is *Vascular Plants of Texas,* by Stanley Jones et al. Unfortunately, the authors do not always agree. The natural result is a certain amount of confusion. This book follows *The Vascular Plants of Texas: A List, Up-dating the Manual of the Vascular Plants of Texas,* second edition, by Marshall C. Johnston.

Those who want to learn more about the plants may refer to several floristic studies (Gillespie 1976; Hartman & Smith 1973; Jones 1975; Lonard, Judd & Sides 1978; Lonard & Judd 1980; Negrete et al. 1999; Richardson 1995). *Aransas: A Naturalist's Guide* and *Matagorda*

Island: A Naturalist's Guide, both by McAlister and McAlister, contain much useful information. The *Manual of the Vascular Plants of Texas,* by Correll and Johnston (1970), describes all the species of plants known to grow in Texas at the time of publication. Britton and Morton's *Shore Ecology of the Gulf of Mexico* (1989) provides useful detail regarding the topography, soils, etc.

ABOUT BOTANICAL TERMS

Botanical terms are often long and difficult to pronounce and spell. Many of them can be replaced by ordinary English words or phrases, and this has been done when possible. However, some terms have no convenient English words or short phrases. This is especially true for leaf and flower characteristics. The major ones are illustrated below.

THE LEAF PARTS

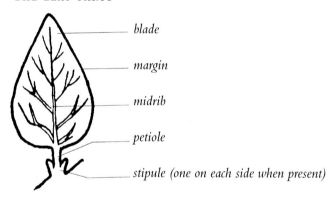

blade

margin

midrib

petiole

stipule (one on each side when present)

LEAVES CAN BE SIMPLE OR COMPOUND

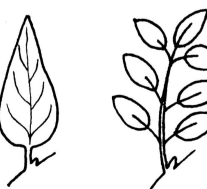

Simple   *Pinnately Compound*   *Palmately Compound*

A COMPOUND LEAF CAN BE ONE, TWO, OR MORE TIMES COMPOUND

Once Compound

Twice Compound

Three Times Compound

LEAF ARRANGEMENT ON THE STEM

Alternate

Opposite

Whorled

SOME COMMON LEAF SHAPES

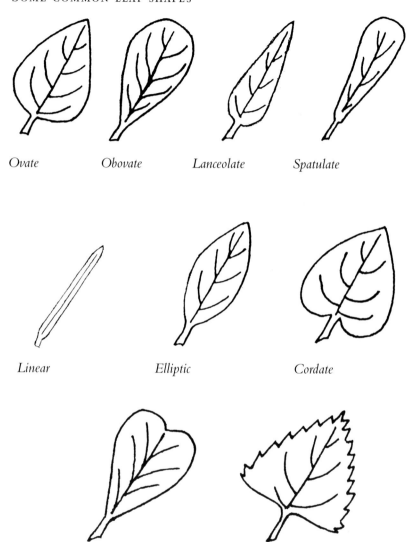

Ovate   Obovate   Lanceolate   Spatulate

Linear   Elliptic   Cordate

Obcordate   Triangular

LEAF MARGINS

The edge (margin) of the leaf can be perfectly smooth (entire), or with various irregularities. Leaves that have different kinds of small cuts into the margin have many different descriptive terms. For convenience, all these terms are "lumped" into one category, "toothed." In the same way, leaves with various larger cuts into the margin are called "lobed."

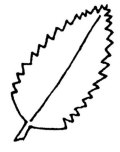

Entire *Toothed*

Lobed

THE PARTS OF A FLOWER

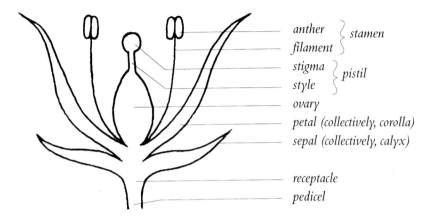

anther ⎫ *stamen*
filament ⎭

stigma ⎫ *pistil*
style ⎭

ovary

petal (collectively, corolla)

sepal (collectively, calyx)

receptacle

pedicel

POSITION OF THE OVARY

An ovary is called superior if the other flower parts are joined to the receptacle below the ovary. It is called inferior if the other parts are joined to the ovary itself, or above it.

Ovary Superior   *Ovary Inferior*

The Compositae family

The Compositae family (also called Asteraceae or Sunflower family) has a unique flower arrangement that merits special attention. Using the common sunflower for an example, each of the yellow "petals" is a flower, and is called a ray flower (or ray floret). Each of the tiny brown dots in the center is also a flower, and is called a disk flower (or disk floret). The sunflower, then, is a composite of many flowers on a common receptacle; hence the name Compositae. The cluster of florets on one receptacle is called a "head." There is much variation of this pattern, and not all members of the family have both ray and disk florets. Each of the green parts at the base of the sunflower is called a phyllary. All the phyllaries together are called the involucre.

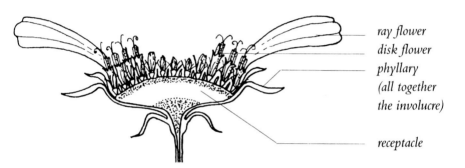

ray flower

disk flower

phyllary
(all together
the involucre)

receptacle

The sunflower "seed" is actually a fruit, called an achene. It has a pair of tiny points at the top. Other members of the family have a plumelike top, which you have probably seen illustrated in pictures of a dandelion. This top part of the fruit, in both cases mentioned, is called the pappus.

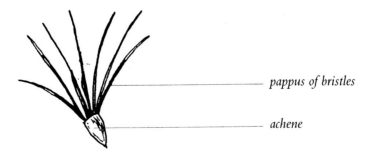

pappus of bristles

achene

Wildflowers
and Other
Plants
of Texas
Beaches
and Islands

Cat Tail

FAMILY: Typhaceae

SCIENTIFIC NAME: *Typha domingensis*

STEMS: Creeping, below ground.

LEAVES: Very tall and narrow, up to 8' tall.

FLOWERS: Minute, in dense, cylindrical brown clusters. The male flowers are in a cluster at the top, and just below that is the cluster of female flowers.

FRUIT: Tiny, inconspicuous.

HABITAT: Moist or wet places, Boca Chica Beach; Brazos, Padre, and Matagorda Islands.

BLOOM PERIOD: Summer.

COMMENTS: *Typha latifolia* (Common Cat Tail) also grows on the coast. In this species, there is no space between the male and female flowers. In *T. domingensis,* the male and female flowers are separated by a short space.

In the upper cluster the flowers are male, and the lower ones are female.

Burhead

FAMILY: Alismataceae
SCIENTIFIC NAME: *Echinodorus rostratus*
STEMS: Erect, up to 2' tall.
LEAVES: In basal rosettes. Blades broad, ovate, up to 8" long, sometimes as broad.
FLOWERS: In whorls, white, with 3 petals and 3 sepals, up to ¾" broad.
FRUIT: Spiny, elliptical.
HABITAT: Near water or recently dried water holes. Probably on all the Texas coast. Not abundant.
BLOOM PERIOD: Spring and summer.
COMMENTS: Also known as *Echinodorus berteroi* or *Echinodorus beteroi*.

Arrowhead

FAMILY: Alismataceae
SCIENTIFIC NAME: *Sagittaria longiloba*
STEMS: None visible.
LEAVES: More or less erect, 2'–3' tall. Blades arrowhead-shaped, up to about 12" long.
FLOWERS: Mostly unisexual, ⅝"–1¼" broad, the petals white to pink.
FRUIT: Very small achenes, less than ⅛" long.
HABITAT: Shallow water or mud, Galveston Island.
BLOOM PERIOD: Spring, summer, fall.

Bushy Bluestem

FAMILY: Gramineae
SCIENTIFIC NAME: *Andropogon glomeratus*
STEMS: Erect, up to 51" tall.
LEAVES: Blades flat, up to 14" long and
¼" broad.
FLOWERS: Very tiny, apical.
FRUIT: Inconspicuous. The long awns on
the bracts enclosing the fruit give the
fruiting stalk a cottony appearance.
HABITAT: Moist places, sandy clay, Brazos,
Padre, Mustang, and Matagorda Islands.
BLOOM PERIOD: Fall.

Giant Reed

FAMILY: Gramineae
SCIENTIFIC NAME: *Arundo donax*
STEMS: Erect, hollow, unbranched, up to 13' tall.
LEAVES: Strap-shaped, up to 18" long and 1" broad, with sheaths around the stem.
FLOWERS: Very tiny, in large apical clusters.
FRUIT: None.
HABITAT: Near water, Padre Island.
BLOOM PERIOD: Summer, fall.
COMMENTS: An introduced plant. According to Cheatham and Johnston (1995), this is the species that is used to make reeds for woodwind instruments.

Buffel Grass

FAMILY: Gramineae
SCIENTIFIC NAME: *Cenchrus ciliaris*
STEMS: Erect or bending, up to 40" tall.
LEAVES: Blades up to 10" long.
FLOWERS: Very tiny, apical.
FRUIT: Inconspicuous, enclosed in bracts.
The fruiting stalk resembles a cluster of
sandburs, but the burrs are soft.
HABITAT: Sandy clay, Brazos Island.
BLOOM PERIOD: All seasons.
COMMENTS: Also known as *Pennisetum
ciliare.*

Sandbur

FAMILY: Gramineae
SCIENTIFIC NAME: *Cenchrus incertus*
STEMS: Erect, up to 30" tall.
LEAVES: Up to 8" long and ¼" broad.
FLOWERS: Very tiny, apical.
FRUIT: The typical sandburs.
HABITAT: Throughout the Texas beaches.
BLOOM PERIOD: All seasons.
COMMENTS: The burrs are dispersed by
sticking to clothing or animal fur. Each
burr contains a seed.

Also known as *Cenchrus spinifex.*

Hooded Windmill Grass

FAMILY: Gramineae
SCIENTIFIC NAME: *Chloris cucullata*
STEMS: Erect or bending, up to 24" tall.
LEAVES: Mostly basal, up to 8" long and about ⅛" broad.
FLOWERS: Very tiny, apical.
FRUIT: Inconspicuous, in apical threadlike branches that originate from more or less the same point on the major axis.
HABITAT: Brazos, Padre, Mustang, and Matagorda Islands.
BLOOM PERIOD: Spring, summer, fall.

Canada Wild Rye

FAMILY: Gramineae
SCIENTIFIC NAME: *Elymus canadensis*
STEMS: Leaning, about 30"– 60" tall.
LEAVES: Widely separated along the stems;
narrow, flat, or folded; 6" long or more.
FLOWERS: Tiny, in tight, apical bloom
stalks, with long, threadlike extensions
from each floret.
FRUIT: Small, in apical clusters.
HABITAT: Bolivar Peninsula, in sandy clay
near the bay.
BLOOM PERIOD: Spring, summer.

Fruiting spike

Red Lovegrass

FAMILY: Gramineae
SCIENTIFIC NAME: *Eragrostis secundiflora*
subsp. *oxylepis*
STEMS: Erect, up to 30" tall.
LEAVES: Up to 6" long and ⅛" broad.
FLOWERS: Tiny, in apical clusters.
FRUIT: Tiny, in apical clusters, hidden by
bracts, which often turn a reddish-purple
color.
HABITAT: Brazos and Padre Islands.
BLOOM PERIOD: Spring, summer, fall.

Flowering spike

Shoregrass

FAMILY: Gramineae
SCIENTIFIC NAME: *Monanthochloë littoralis*
STEMS: Creeping, forming mats.
LEAVES: Up to ⁹⁄₁₆" long, stiff and sharp-pointed.
FLOWERS: Tiny, in the leaf axils.
FRUIT: Inconspicuous.
HABITAT: Moist places, especially along the bay shores, throughout the Texas beaches.
BLOOM PERIOD: Spring.
COMMENTS: This grass is very abundant and easy to recognize, with its sharp leaves and its habit of growing in mats.

Gulfdune Paspalum

FAMILY: Gramineae

SCIENTIFIC NAME: *Paspalum monostachyum*

STEMS: Erect, up to 44" tall.

LEAVES: Up to 12" long and ⅛" broad.

FLOWERS: Tiny, all on one side of an apical bloom stalk.

FRUIT: Small, hidden by bracts, arranged all on one side of the fruiting stalk.

HABITAT: Throughout the Texas beaches.

BLOOM PERIOD: Fall.

COMMENTS: The arrangement of the fruit all on one side of the fruiting stalk makes it a little easier to recognize this genus.

Flowering spike

Common Reed

FAMILY: Gramineae
SCIENTIFIC NAME: *Phragmites australis*
STEMS: Erect, 6½'–13' tall.
LEAVES: Up to 20" long and 2" broad.
FLOWERS: Tiny, in dense apical clusters.
FRUIT: Tiny, hidden by bracts, in dense apical clusters.
HABITAT: Boca Chica Beach, Brazos Island, and Padre Island.
BLOOM PERIOD: Summer, fall.
COMMENTS: This is one of the two tallest grass species of the Texas coast. *Arundo donax,* sometimes growing a little taller, is found on Padre Island. Its leaf sheaths (the part of the leaf that wraps around the stem) are rough on the edges, while those of *P. australis* are smooth.

Seacoast Bluestem

FAMILY: Gramineae
SCIENTIFIC NAME: *Schizachyrium scoparium*
STEMS: Erect, up to 32" tall.
LEAVES: 10" or longer.
FLOWERS: Very tiny, apical.
FRUIT: Very small, apical, hidden by bracts.
HABITAT: Abundant, throughout the Texas beaches.
BLOOM PERIOD: Fall and early winter.
COMMENTS: The many hairs on the inflorescence and fruiting stalk give these plants a silvery glow in the sunlight.

Bristle Grass

FAMILY: Gramineae
SCIENTIFIC NAME: *Setaria scheelei*
STEMS: Leaning, up to 48" tall, generally much shorter.
LEAVES: Up to 12" long and ¾" broad.
FLOWERS: Tiny, in bristly apical clusters shaped like a cylinder tapering to a point.
FRUIT: Very small, in bristly clusters shaped like a cylinder tapering to a point.
HABITAT: Padre Island.
BLOOM PERIOD: Spring, summer, fall.

Johnson Grass

FAMILY: Gramineae
SCIENTIFIC NAME: *Sorghum halepense*
STEMS: Erect or leaning, 2'–5' tall.
LEAVES: Up to 30" long and ¾" broad.
FLOWERS: Tiny, in loose apical clusters.

FRUIT: Very small, enclosed in bracts in loose apical clusters.
HABITAT: Padre and Mustang Islands.
BLOOM PERIOD: All seasons.

Flowering spike

Marshhay Cordgrass

FAMILY: Gramineae
SCIENTIFIC NAME: *Spartina patens*
STEMS: Erect, 28"–48" tall.
LEAVES: Up to 28" long.
FLOWERS: Tiny, apical.
FRUIT: Very small, apical, enclosed by bracts.
HABITAT: Boca Chica Beach, Brazos Island.
BLOOM PERIOD: Summer, fall.

Flowering spike

Gulf Cordgrass

FAMILY: Gramineae
SCIENTIFIC NAME: *Spartina spartinae*
STEMS: Erect, forming large clumps
24"–52" tall.
LEAVES: Up to 36" long. The tips are hard
and sharp-pointed.
FLOWERS: Tiny, apical.
FRUIT: Very small, apical, enclosed by
bracts.
HABITAT: Throughout the Texas coast.
BLOOM PERIOD: Spring, summer, fall.
COMMENTS: Gulf Cordgrass is usually
abundant where it occurs.

Flowering spike

Seashore Dropseed

FAMILY: Gramineae
SCIENTIFIC NAME: *Sporobolus virginicus*
STEMS: Leaning, falling over, and rooting at the nodes, up to 18" tall.
LEAVES: Up to 4" long and ⅛" broad.
FLOWERS: Tiny, apical.
FRUIT: Very small, apical, enclosed in bracts.
HABITAT: Throughout the Texas beaches.
BLOOM PERIOD: Summer and fall.

Sea Oats

FAMILY: Gramineae
SCIENTIFIC NAME: *Uniola paniculata*
STEMS: Erect, mostly 4'–7' tall.
LEAVES: Up to 32" long and ⅜" broad.
FLOWERS: Tiny, apical.
FRUIT: Very small, in apical clusters resembling the fruiting stalk of oats.
HABITAT: Sand dunes, throughout the Texas beaches.
BLOOM PERIOD: Summer, fall.
COMMENTS: Sea oats is probably the best-known grass of the Texas beaches. It is often seen in photographs and paintings depicting the Gulf coast.

Flat Sedge

FAMILY: Cyperaceae
SCIENTIFIC NAME: *Cyperus tenuis*
STEMS: Erect, up to 32" tall.
LEAVES: Narrow and grasslike.
FLOWERS: Very tiny, in flattened clusters called spikelets.
FRUIT: Very small, 3-cornered achenes.
HABITAT: Moist sand, Boca Chica Beach.
BLOOM PERIOD: Summer, fall.
COMMENTS: Also known as *Cyperus thyrsiflorus.*

Other *Cyperus* reported on the barrier islands are *C. brevifolius, C. croceus, C. echinatus, C. elegans, C. esculentus, C. globulosus, C. haspan, C. ochraceus, C. ovularis, C. polystachyos, C. pseudothyrsiflorus, C. retroflexus, C. retrorsus, C. rotundus, C. setigerus, C. squarosus, C. strigosus, C. surinamensis, C. uniflorus,* and *C. virens.* They are difficult to distinguish without a good key and a strong hand lens or microscope.

White-Topped Umbrella Grass

FAMILY: Cyperaceae
SCIENTIFIC NAME: *Dichromena colorata*
STEMS: Erect, up to 22" tall.
LEAVES: Narrow and grasslike.
FLOWERS: Very tiny at the top of the plant, subtended by white leaflike bracts.
FRUIT: Very small, flattened, 2-edged achenes.
HABITAT: Moist places throughout the Texas coast.
BLOOM PERIOD: Summer, fall.
COMMENTS: This is a sedge that is easy to recognize, with its white bracts surrounding the flowers.

Also called *Rhynchospora colorata.*

Spikerush

FAMILY: Cyperaceae

SCIENTIFIC NAME: *Eleocharis obtusa*

STEMS: Erect, up to 20" tall.

LEAVES: Narrow and grasslike.

FLOWERS: Very tiny, in ovoid clusters.

FRUIT: Very small, 2-sided achenes, both sides convex.

HABITAT: Sandy clay, Brazos Island, Boca Chica Beach.

BLOOM PERIOD: Spring, summer.

COMMENTS: Other species of *Eleocharis* reported on the barrier islands are *E. albida, E. atropurpurea, E. cellulosa, E. flavescens, E. geniculata, E. interstincta, E. macrostachya, E. minima, E. montevidensis,* and *E. parvula*. They are distinguished by technical details, and the process can be difficult.

Fimbristylis

FAMILY: Cyperaceae
SCIENTIFIC NAME: *Fimbristylis castanea*
STEMS: Erect, up to 5" tall or more.
LEAVES: Narrow and grasslike.
FLOWERS: Very small, in more or less cylindrical clusters that are rounded apically.
FRUIT: Very small, flattened, 2-edged achenes.
HABITAT: Damp sandy clay or sand, Brazos, Padre, and Matagorda Islands.
BLOOM PERIOD: Summer, fall.

Umbrella Grass

FAMILY: Cyperaceae

SCIENTIFIC NAME: *Fuirena simplex*

STEMS: Erect, up to 20" tall.

LEAVES: Grasslike, narrow, along the stem.

FLOWERS: Very small, in more or less cylindrical clusters that taper to a point.

FRUIT: Very small, 3-cornered achenes.

HABITAT: Boca Chica Beach, Brazos Island, Padre Island.

BLOOM PERIOD: Summer, fall.

COMMENTS: Two varieties are recognized, var. *simplex* and var. *aristulata*. They are difficult to distinguish.

Salt Marsh Bulrush

FAMILY: Cyperaceae
SCIENTIFIC NAME: *Scirpus maritimus* var. *macrostachyus*
STEMS: Erect, up to 40" or taller.
LEAVES: Narrow, grasslike.
FLOWERS: Very small, in conelike clusters. The "cones" are subtended by leaflike bracts that usually point straight outward.
FRUIT: Somewhat flattened achenes, about ⅛" long, brown when mature.

HABITAT: Edge of bay, marshes, Goose Island.
BLOOM PERIOD: Spring, summer, fall.
COMMENTS: This species has several bracts pointing outward from the stem, while *Scirpus pungens* has a single bract pointing upward. *S. californicus, S. koilolepis, S. molestus,* and *S. olneyi* also grow on the coast, usually in moist places.

Also called *Bulboschoenus robustus.*

Bulrush

FAMILY: Cyperaceae
SCIENTIFIC NAME: *Scirpus pungens* var.
longispicatus
STEMS: Erect, up to 5' tall or more.
LEAVES: Narrow and grasslike.
FLOWERS: Very small, in apical clusters
about ⅟₁₆" broad and ⅜" long. The clusters
are subtended by a straight vertical bract
resembling a continuation of the stem.
FRUIT: Flattened, 2-edged achenes, almost
⅛" long.
HABITAT: Brazos and Padre Islands.
BLOOM PERIOD: Spring, summer.
COMMENTS: The genus *Scirpus* is
recognizable by the vertical bract that
subtends the flower clusters, making it
appear as if the flower clusters are
attached several inches below the apex of
the stem. Almost all the species have this
characteristic. Also called *Schoenoplectus
pungens* var. *longispicatus.*

Duckweed

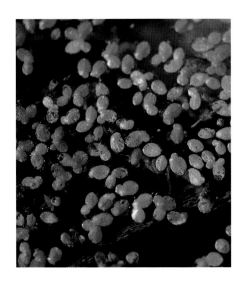

FAMILY: Lemnaceae
SCIENTIFIC NAME: *Lemna* species
STEMS: None.
LEAVES: Tiny, floating, about ¼" long or less.
FLOWERS: Very tiny, reduced.
FRUIT: Minute.
HABITAT: Ponds, canals, lagoons, Galveston Island.
BLOOM PERIOD: Spring, fall.
COMMENTS: *Lemna obscura* and *Wolffia columbiana* have both been seen growing on the Texas coast. *Lemna* has a single root, while *Wolffia* has none. Because of their small size, the different species are very difficult to distinguish. The photograph is of *Lemna minuscula* (also called *L. minuta*), which is similar to *L. obscura*.

Ball Moss

FAMILY: Bromeliaceae
SCIENTIFIC NAME: *Tillandsia recurvata*
STEMS: Small rhizomes are scarcely noticeable. Plants form balls attached to tree limbs.
LEAVES: Gray, curled, up to 4" long.
FLOWERS: Only 1 or 2, violet color, about ¼"–⅜" broad.
FRUIT: A small capsule splitting into 3 parts.
HABITAT: Goose Island. Plants grow attached to tree limbs.
BLOOM PERIOD: Late winter, early spring.
COMMENTS: The common name comes from the growth habit. The plants grow tightly clustered together in balls.

Day Flower

FAMILY: Commelinaceae

SCIENTIFIC NAME: *Commelina elegans*

STEMS: Usually reddish, at first erect, then falling over, rooting at the nodes.

LEAVES: Alternate, ovate to lanceolate, up to 3 ⅛" long.

FLOWERS: Arising from a folded bract, bilateral, with 2 dark blue petals about ¾" broad and 1 much smaller white petal. The flowers usually open in the morning and dissolve by noon.

FRUIT: Small, inconspicuous.

HABITAT: Sandy soil, Boca Chica Beach, Padre Island.

BLOOM PERIOD: All seasons.

COMMENTS: *Commelina elegans* is very similar to *C. erecta,* and is sometimes called *Commelina erecta* var. *elegans.* *C. erecta* has green stems that do not root at the nodes, while *C. elegans* usually has reddish stems that root at the nodes.

Widow's Tears

FAMILY: Commelinaceae
SCIENTIFIC NAME: *Commelina erecta* var.
angustifolia
STEMS: Erect, sometimes falling over.
LEAVES: Alternate, linear to lanceolate, up
to 6" long, usually less.
FLOWERS: Arising from a folded bract,
bilateral with 2 dark blue petals about ¾"
broad, and 1 much smaller white petal.
FRUIT: Small, inconspicuous.
HABITAT: Sand or clay, throughout the
Texas beaches.
BLOOM PERIOD: All seasons.
COMMENTS: The flowers usually open in
the early morning and then dissolve
around noon.

Spiderwort

FAMILY: Commelinaceae
SCIENTIFIC NAME: *Tradescantia micrantha*
STEMS: Creeping, rooting at the nodes.
LEAVES: Alternate, mostly lanceolate, up to
1 ⅜" long.
FLOWERS: Radially symmetrical, the 3
petals rose or pink, ¼" or longer.
FRUIT: Small, inconspicuous.
HABITAT: Sand, sandy clay. Boca Chica
Beach.
BLOOM PERIOD: Spring, summer, fall.
COMMENTS: Also called *Callisia micrantha*.

    Tradescantia micrantha is easily
distinguished from the other beach
Tradescantias by its creeping habit.

Photographed at Lady Bird Johnson Wildflower Center, Austin, Texas

Western Spiderwort

FAMILY: Commelinaceae
SCIENTIFIC NAME: *Tradescantia occidentalis*
STEMS: More or less erect, about 18" tall.
LEAVES: Linear to lanceolate, up to 12"
long.
FLOWERS: Radially symmetrical, up to
1¼" broad, with 3 petals that are variable
in color, violet to pink.
FRUIT: A dry capsule about ³⁄₁₆" long.
HABITAT: Sandy soil, Galveston Island.
BLOOM PERIOD: Spring, summer.
COMMENTS: *Tradescantia humilis* also
grows on the Texas coast. The two species
are easy to distinguish, because *T. humilis*
is hairy and *T. occidentalis* is not.

On both species, the flowers all
originate from the same point at the top
of the bloom spike. They hang downward,
reminiscent of the shape of a spider.

Water Stargrass

FAMILY: Pontederiaceae
SCIENTIFIC NAME: *Heteranthera liebmannii*
STEMS: Absent or elongate and branching under water.
LEAVES: In a rosette, linear, up to 6" long.
FLOWERS: Yellow, about ¾" broad, reaching above the water surface.
FRUIT: Tiny, inconspicuous.
HABITAT: Wet places, Padre Island.
BLOOM PERIOD: Spring, summer.
COMMENTS: Water Stargrass grows either submerged in water or in mud at the edge of a body of water.

Also known as *Heteranthera dubia.*

Crow Poison

FAMILY: Liliaceae
SCIENTIFIC NAME: *Nothoscordum bivalve*
STEMS: None.
LEAVES: Linear, up to 20" long,
resembling onion leaves but without the
scent.
FLOWERS: White, in clusters up to 12.
Petals up to 1" long.
FRUIT: A capsule about ¼" long, splitting
into 3 parts.
HABITAT: Sandy soil, Boca Chica Beach,
Brazos and Padre Islands.
BLOOM PERIOD: All seasons.

Common Greenbrier

FAMILY: Liliaceae
SCIENTIFIC NAME: *Smilax bona-nox*
STEMS: Vines, usually with tendrils; the
lower parts prickly, the upper parts with
or without prickles.
LEAVES: Alternate, variable in shape, with
3 major veins arising from the blade base.
FLOWERS: Small, greenish or whitish, in
umbrella-like clusters. Male and female
flowers on separate plants.
FRUIT: A berry, black when mature, about
¼" broad, containing 1 seed.
HABITAT: Goose Island.
BLOOM PERIOD: Spring to early summer.

Flower buds

Spanish Dagger, Palma Pita

FAMILY: Liliaceae

SCIENTIFIC NAME: *Yucca treculeana*

STEMS: Woody, branched, up to 12' tall.

LEAVES: Simple, crowded in a spiral around the stem, up to 40" long, stiff and spine-tipped.

FLOWERS: In apical clusters. Sepals 3 and petals 3, white, looking alike, up to 1¾" long.

FRUIT: A dry capsule up to 4" long.

HABITAT: Various soils, Brazos, Padre, and Matagorda Islands.

BLOOM PERIOD: Spring.

COMMENTS: The flowers are often collected and eaten. *Yucca constricta* is reported for Padre Island. Its broadest leaves are about ¾" wide; the leaves of *Y. treculeana* are 1⅜" or wider.

Century Plant

FAMILY: Agavaceae
SCIENTIFIC NAME: *Agave americana*
STEMS: Hidden by the large leaves.
LEAVES: Thick and succulent, crowded in
a spiral, gray with whitish marks, toothed
on the margins with a sharp apical spine,
up to 66" long.
FLOWERS: Greenish-yellow, at the top of
tall stalks up to 22' or taller.
FRUIT: A dry capsule.
HABITAT: Brazos Island, between dunes
and the Laguna Madre.
BLOOM PERIOD: Summer.
COMMENTS: This plant is often cultivated.
Century plants have been used as a source
of fiber and food, and for making
alcoholic beverages.

Rainlily

FAMILY: Amaryllidaceae

SCIENTIFIC NAME: *Cooperia drummondii*

STEMS: Inconspicuous, part of the underground bulbs.

LEAVES: 2–5, up to 12" tall and ¼" broad.

FLOWERS: Petals and sepals white, up to ¾" long, with a long tube up to 4¾" long.

FRUIT: A dry capsule.

HABITAT: Widespread, in sand/clay soils, Brazos, Padre, Mustang, and Matagorda Islands.

BLOOM PERIOD: Rainlilies often bloom after rains, especially in summer.

COMMENTS: Gardeners often cultivate different species of rainlilies for their color and their interesting habit of blooming after rains.

Blue-Eyed Grass

FAMILY: Iridaceae
SCIENTIFIC NAME: *Sisyrinchium biforme*
STEMS: Erect, up to 18" tall.
LEAVES: Folded, in 2 rows, elongate and about ⅛" broad.
FLOWERS: Petals and sepals light blue, about ⅜" long.
FRUIT: An erect cylindrical capsule about ¼" tall.
HABITAT: Low places, Brazos, Padre, and Matagorda Islands.
BLOOM PERIOD: Mostly spring and summer.

Spring Ladies' Tresses

FAMILY: Orchidaceae
SCIENTIFIC NAME: *Spiranthes vernalis*
STEMS: None.
LEAVES: Simple, linear, up to 6" long.
FLOWERS: Bilaterally symmetrical, white, about ⅜" long, produced on a bloom stalk 18" tall or less.
FRUIT: A small capsule.
HABITAT: Sandy areas, Boca Chica Beach, Brazos, Padre, and Matagorda Islands.
BLOOM PERIOD: Spring.
COMMENTS: This is the only native orchid in the southernmost part of Texas.

Black Willow

FAMILY: Salicaceae
SCIENTIFIC NAME: *Salix nigra*
STEMS: Deciduous trees up to 30' tall or more.
LEAVES: Alternate, lanceolate, up to 4¾" long, the margins with very tiny teeth.
FLOWERS: Very tiny, unisexual, male and female flowers on separate plants.
FRUIT: A capsule about ¼" long, bearing seeds with silky hairs.
HABITAT: Padre Island, Goose Island.
BLOOM PERIOD: Spring and summer.
COMMENTS: The twigs are sometimes soaked in water to produce a fluid that promotes root growth in stem cuttings.

Live Oak

FAMILY: Fagaceae

SCIENTIFIC NAME: *Quercus virginiana*

STEMS: Trees up to 40' tall or more. The bark is dark brown or black and deeply furrowed.

LEAVES: Alternate and simple, thick and stiff, from elliptic to ovate, up to 4¾" long, the margins often toothed.

FLOWERS: Male and female flowers on the same tree. The male flowers are tiny, reduced, in clusters (catkins). The female flowers are single or a few in a cluster.

FRUIT: An acorn (a nut seated in a cup of scales), up to 1⅛" long.

HABITAT: Sandy soil, Padre, Goose, Matagorda, and Galveston Islands.

BLOOM PERIOD: Spring.

COMMENTS: Other oaks found on the coast are *Q. hemisphaerica, Q. marilandica,* and *Q. minima.*

Hackberry, Sugarberry, Palo Blanco

FAMILY: Ulmaceae

SCIENTIFIC NAME: *Celtis laevigata*

STEMS: Trees up to 90' or taller. The trunk is mottled whitish/gray, usually with wartlike bumps.

LEAVES: Ovate to variable, up to 3¼" long, usually asymmetric, sometimes noticeably rough when rubbed from tip to petiole.

FLOWERS: Very small, inconspicuous.

FRUIT: Roundish, orange or brown drupes (sometimes called berries) about ⁵⁄₁₆" broad.

HABITAT: Sandy soils, Goose Island.

BLOOM PERIOD: Spring.

COMMENTS: This tree is widespread in Texas. It is most easily recognized by its whitish, warty trunk. The drupes are sweet and are sometimes used to make jelly.

Stinging Weed

FAMILY: Urticaceae
SCIENTIFIC NAME: *Urtica chamaedryoides*
STEMS: Erect, up to 24" tall, juicy, with stinging hairs.
LEAVES: Lance-shaped to ovate, about 2⅜" long, with stinging hairs.
FLOWERS: White, about ⅛" broad, in small clusters from the leaf axils.
FRUIT: A very small achene.
HABITAT: Sandy clay, Padre, Mustang, and Matagorda Islands.
BLOOM PERIOD: Spring, summer.
COMMENTS: A touch to any part of the plant causes an unpleasant burning sensation.

Wild Buckwheat

FAMILY: Polygonaceae
SCIENTIFIC NAME: *Eriogonum multiflorum*
STEMS: Densely hairy, erect, up to 6' tall.
LEAVES: Densely hairy, the blades lanceolate to ovate, up to 3⅛" long.
FLOWERS: Tiny, white to tan, in clusters surrounded by cuplike structures about ⅛" broad.
FRUIT: Tiny, 1-seeded.
HABITAT: Sandy soils, Padre, Mustang, and Matagorda Islands.
BLOOM PERIOD: Summer, fall.

Dock

FAMILY: Polygonaceae
SCIENTIFIC NAME: *Rumex chrysocarpus*
STEMS: Erect, sometimes falling over, up to 28" tall, often reddish.
LEAVES: Alternate, the blades mostly lanceolate, up to 4¾" long.
FLOWERS: Tiny, enclosed in bracts.
FRUIT: Less than ⅛" tall, enclosed in the reddish-brown inflated sepals, which are about 3⁄16" long.
HABITAT: Various soils, moist places, Padre and Matagorda Islands.
BLOOM PERIOD: Spring, summer, fall.

Spiny-Fruited Saltbush

FAMILY: Chenopodiaceae
SCIENTIFIC NAME: *Atriplex acanthocarpa*
STEMS: Erect branching shrubs to 3' or taller.
LEAVES: Mostly alternate, silver-gray, the blades arrowhead-shaped, up to 2⅜" long.
FLOWERS: Tiny, in small knots, inconspicuous.
FRUIT: Spiny, up to ⅝" long.
HABITAT: Alkaline sand or clay, Padre Island.
BLOOM PERIOD: Spring, summer, fall.
COMMENTS: Several other species of *Atriplex* are reported to grow on Texas beaches and islands. Usually they are difficult to distinguish. *A. acanthocarpa* is easily recognized by its spiny fruit.

Quelite

FAMILY: Chenopodiaceae

SCIENTIFIC NAME: *Atriplex arenaria*

STEMS: Erect to prostrate, up to 20" tall.

LEAVES: Alternate, oblanceolate to oblong, gray-green or silvery, up to 1" long.

FLOWERS: Tiny; male and female flowers on the same plant. The male flowers are in cylindrical clusters on the upper part of the plant. The female flowers are in the axils of the lower leaves.

FRUIT: Small, covered with bracts up to ⅛" long. The bracts are spiny on the margins and the sides.

HABITAT: Alkaline soils, Boca Chica Beach, Padre and Matagorda Islands.

BLOOM PERIOD: Spring, summer, fall.

COMMENTS: *Atriplex pentandra* and *A. semibaccata* also grow on the Texas coast. While the stems of *A. arenaria* grow erect, *A. semibaccata* grows more or less prostrate. *A. pentandra* is sometimes listed as a synonym of *A. arenaria*. There are small differences between them that require a microscope to distinguish.

A. acanthocarpa and *A. matamorensis* are distinctive enough to be more easily recognized by the characteristics mentioned in the Comments for each species.

Matamoros Saltbush

FAMILY: Chenopodiaceae
SCIENTIFIC NAME: *Atriplex matamorensis*
STEMS: Erect, up to 24" tall.
LEAVES: Mostly opposite, silver-gray, very narrow and crowded, up to ¼" long.
FLOWERS: Tiny, in small knots, inconspicuous.
FRUIT: Inconspicuous, less than ⅛" long.
HABITAT: Sandy clay, Padre and Matagorda Islands.
BLOOM PERIOD: Spring, summer, fall.
COMMENTS: Matamoros Saltbush is distinguished from the other species of *Atriplex* by its crowded, narrow leaves.

Pitseed Goosefoot

FAMILY: Chenopodiaceae
SCIENTIFIC NAME: *Chenopodium berlandieri*
STEMS: Erect, up to 5' tall.
LEAVES: Usually ill-scented when crushed, the blades ovate, up to 1½" long.
FLOWERS: Tiny, mealy, in small clusters.
FRUIT: Very small, 1-seeded.
HABITAT: Widespread.
BLOOM PERIOD: Spring, summer, fall.
COMMENTS: *Chenopodium ambrosioides* and *C. incanum* are also reported to grow on the Texas coast. *C. ambrosioides* is distinguished from the other two by the presence of hairs and glands. The other two species are hairless. The leaf blades of *C. incanum* have basal lobes, while those of *C. berlandieri* do not.

Glasswort

FAMILY: Chenopodiaceae
SCIENTIFIC NAME: *Salicornia bigelovii*
STEMS: Fleshy, erect, up to 12" or taller.
LEAVES: Opposite, scalelike, tightly hugging the stem.
FLOWERS: Minute, barely emerging beyond the edge of the clasping leaf.
FRUIT: Inconspicuous, 1-seeded.
HABITAT: Throughout the Texas beaches, in sand.
BLOOM PERIOD: All seasons.
COMMENTS: The erect growth of *Salicornia bigelovii* distinguishes it from *S. virginica,* which grows prostrate.

Single plant, in flower

Glasswort

FAMILY: Chenopodiaceae
SCIENTIFIC NAME: *Salicornia virginica*
STEMS: Fleshy, prostrate.
LEAVES: Opposite, scalelike, tightly
hugging the stem.
FLOWERS: Minute, barely emerging
beyond the edge of the clasping leaf.
FRUIT: Inconspicuous, 1-seeded.
HABITAT: Reported on Padre, Brazos, and
Matagorda Islands, probably widespread.
BLOOM PERIOD: Spring, summer, fall.
COMMENTS: The two *Salicornia* species are
very similar. It is especially easy to confuse
them when the erect-growing *S. bigelovii*
falls over, imitating the prostrate growth
of *S. virginica*.

Sea Blite

FAMILY: Chenopodiaceae

SCIENTIFIC NAME: *Suaeda linearis*

STEMS: Fleshy, low-growing, erect or falling over.

LEAVES: Fleshy, nearly cylindrical, hairless, green, often turning purple.

FLOWERS: Tiny, inconspicuous.

FRUIT: Inconspicuous, with a single black seed.

HABITAT: Throughout the Texas beaches.

BLOOM PERIOD: Spring, summer, fall.

COMMENTS: *Suaeda conferta, S. calceofiliformis, S. moquinii,* and *S. tampicensis* also grow on the barrier islands. Generally the species cannot be distinguished without a microscope or a hand lens.

Suaeda

FAMILY: Chenopodiaceae
SCIENTIFIC NAME: *Suaeda tampicensis*
STEMS: Erect to falling over, branching.
LEAVES: Alternate, fleshy, cylindrical, up to
⅝" long.
FLOWERS: Tiny, inconspicuous.
FRUIT: Inconspicuous, with a single black
seed.
HABITAT: Salty, sandy soils, Padre Island.
BLOOM PERIOD: Spring, summer, fall.
COMMENTS: The hairy stems of this
species distinguish it from the other
Suaedas.

Fleshy-Leaved Amaranthus

FAMILY: Amaranthaceae

SCIENTIFIC NAME: *Amaranthus greggii*

STEMS: Erect or sprawling, mostly hairless.

LEAVES: Alternate, thick and fleshy, up to 5¼" long.

FLOWERS: Tiny, scalelike, mostly in terminal bloom stalks. Male and female flowers on separate plants.

FRUIT: Inconspicuous.

HABITAT: Loose sand, on front side and lee side of dunes. Reported on Boca Chica Beach and Padre Island; probably much more widespread.

BLOOM PERIOD: All seasons.

COMMENTS: Sereno Watson described this species in 1877 from a specimen collected in 1847 near the mouth of the Rio Grande.

Amaranthus greggii is distinguished from the other beach species by its thick and fleshy leaves.

Palmer Amaranth

FAMILY: Amaranthaceae

SCIENTIFIC NAME: *Amaranthus palmeri*

STEMS: Stout, erect, usually about 39" tall, rarely up to 6' or taller.

LEAVES: Petioles as long as the blades, the blades up to 3" long.

FLOWERS: Tiny, scalelike, in slender terminal bloom stalks or in clusters along the stem. Male and female flowers on separate plants.

FRUIT: Inconspicuous.

HABITAT: Widespread on disturbed areas.

BLOOM PERIOD: All seasons.

COMMENTS: *Amaranthus palmeri* resembles two other beach species, *A. arenicola* and *A. viridis*. *A. viridis* has flowers of both sexes on the same plant. Plants of the other two species are unisexual. Examination with a microscope or good hand lens shows the corolla parts of *A. palmeri* are tapered and spinelike, while those of *A. arenicola* are not spinelike. Another beach species, *A. spinosus,* is recognized by the spines in its leaf axils.

Florida Snake Cotton

FAMILY: Amaranthaceae
SCIENTIFIC NAME: *Froelichia floridana*
STEMS: Erect, 3' or taller.
LEAVES: Alternate, elliptic or somewhat broader basally.
FLOWERS: Tiny, tightly packed.
FRUIT: Woolly, tightly packed.
HABITAT: Deep sand, Mustang Island.
BLOOM PERIOD: Spring, summer, fall.
COMMENTS: The common name of Snake Cotton comes from the cottony appearance of the tightly packed fruit.

Globe Amaranth

FAMILY: Amaranthaceae
SCIENTIFIC NAME: *Gomphrena nealleyi*
STEMS: Erect, leaning, or falling over, 4"–12" long, hairy.
LEAVES: Opposite, without petioles, ¾"–1½" long.
FLOWERS: Tiny, crowded, and concealed by white or pinkish bracts.
FRUIT: Inconspicuous.
HABITAT: Sand or clay, usually in low places. Padre Island, Brazos Island.
BLOOM PERIOD: All seasons.

Silverhead

FAMILY: Amaranthaceae
SCIENTIFIC NAME: *Philoxerus vermicularis*
STEMS: Prostrate, forming mats.
LEAVES: Opposite, without petioles, thick and fleshy, ⅝"–2⅛" long.
FLOWERS: Perfect, in dense cylindric or roundish heads.
FRUIT: Bladderlike, 1-seeded.
HABITAT: In sand, throughout the Texas coast.
BLOOM PERIOD: All seasons.
COMMENTS: Silverhead forms large mats that are conspicuous because of their bright silver color.
 Also known as *Blutaparon vermiculare*.

Espanta Vaqueros

FAMILY: Amaranthaceae

SCIENTIFIC NAME: *Tidestromia lanuginosa*

STEMS: Erect or prostrate, up to 6" tall, hairy.

LEAVES: Opposite, gray-green to whitish, hairy, the blades broadly ovate, up to 1¼" long.

FLOWERS: Inconspicuous, in axillary clusters.

FRUIT: Inconspicuous.

HABITAT: Common in sand throughout the Texas coast.

BLOOM PERIOD: Spring, summer, fall.

COMMENTS: Because these plants are usually whitish and bright, they are usually quite conspicuous.

Scarlet Spiderling

FAMILY: Nyctaginaceae
SCIENTIFIC NAME: *Boerhaavia coccinea*
STEMS: Leaning or prostrate, up to 4' long.
LEAVES: Opposite, sticky from the numerous glands. Blades roundish to ovate, up to 2⅛" long.
FLOWERS: Tiny, red, in clusters of 2 to 4.
FRUIT: 1-seeded, leathery, and glandular.
HABITAT: Various, Padre, Mustang, and Matagorda Islands.
BLOOM PERIOD: Spring, summer, fall.

White Four O'Clock

FAMILY: Nyctaginaceae
SCIENTIFIC NAME: *Mirabilis albida*
STEMS: Erect, up to 42" or taller, swollen at the nodes.
LEAVES: Opposite, succulent. Blades lanceolate to ovate, up to 4¾" long.
FLOWERS: Rose-colored to whitish, up to ⅜" long, in groups of 3, which are partially enclosed in 5 fused bracts.
FRUIT: About ⅛" tall. The fused bracts become enlarged and papery to partially enclose the fruit.
HABITAT: Sandy soil, Boca Chica Beach, Brazos Island, and Padre Island.
BLOOM PERIOD: All seasons.

Vidrillos

FAMILY: Bataceae
SCIENTIFIC NAME: *Batis maritima*
STEMS: Long and creeping.
LEAVES: Yellowish, succulent, opposite, cylindrical.
FLOWERS: Insignificant, crowded in the leaf axils.
FRUIT: Insignificant.
HABITAT: Salty soils, especially near water or where water stands for long periods of time. Common along the Texas coast.
BLOOM PERIOD: Spring, summer, fall.
COMMENTS: Vidrillos is usually abundant where it grows. The yellowish color of the leaves makes the plant quite noticeable.

Pokeweed

FAMILY: Phytolaccaceae
SCIENTIFIC NAME: *Phytolacca americana*
STEMS: Erect, up to 5' or taller.
LEAVES: Alternate, the blades more or less lanceolate, 4"–10" long, with prominent veins. Sometimes the leaves have a purplish color.
FLOWERS: Small, white, in clusters.
FRUIT: Dark purple, roundish berries, ⅜" broad or more.
HABITAT: Goose Island, Galveston Island.
BLOOM PERIOD: Summer, fall.
COMMENTS: The leaves are usually green with whitish veins, but some plants have purple coloring, especially in the veins.

Photographed at Lady Bird Johnson Wildflower Center, Austin, Texas

Pigeonberry

FAMILY: Phytolaccaceae
SCIENTIFIC NAME: *Rivina humilis*
STEMS: Erect, up to 3' tall, usually shorter. Occasionally sprawling.
LEAVES: Alternate, blades ovate, up to 6" long.

FLOWERS: Small, pink, in clusters.
FRUIT: A red, roundish berry about ⅛" broad.
HABITAT: Goose, Matagorda, and Galveston Islands.
BLOOM PERIOD: All seasons.

Cenicilla

FAMILY: Aizoaceae
SCIENTIFIC NAME: *Sesuvium portulacastrum*
STEMS: Prostrate, rooting at the nodes.
LEAVES: Opposite, succulent, up to 2⅜"
long.
FLOWERS: Solitary, pink, about 1⅛" broad,
with 5 sepals.
FRUIT: Inconspicuous.
HABITAT: Common in beach sands and
bay areas throughout the Texas beaches.
BLOOM PERIOD: Almost all seasons. Time
out for extreme cold weather.
COMMENTS: This is one of the few species
that grows on the front side of the dunes.
The flowers are unusual in that there are
no petals. The brightly colored parts are
the sepals.

The fleshy, succulent leaves distinguish
this species from the other beach species.

Sea Purslane

FAMILY: Aizoaceae
SCIENTIFIC NAME: *Sesuvium sessile*
STEMS: Prostrate, spreading by rhizomes.
LEAVES: Almost linear in shape, somewhat
succulent, and up to 1¼" long.
FLOWERS: Solitary, pink, about ¾" broad,
with 5 sepals.
FRUIT: Inconspicuous.
HABITAT: Soils of sandy clay, Padre Island.
BLOOM PERIOD: Almost all seasons.
COMMENTS: *Sesuvium verrucosum,* which
also grows on our beaches, has stems that
are erect or leaning, sometimes falling
over. *S. maritimum* is distinguished by its
smooth seeds.

Horse Purslane

FAMILY: Aizoaceae
SCIENTIFIC NAME: *Trianthema
portulacastrum*
STEMS: Prostrate, the ends rising upward.
LEAVES: Opposite, succulent, with
stipules. Blades ovate, up to 1½" long.
FLOWERS: Solitary, petals pink, ⅜" broad
or less. Petals absent.
FRUIT: Inconspicuous.
HABITAT: Various soils, Padre Island.
BLOOM PERIOD: Summer, fall.

Common Purslane

FAMILY: Portulacaceae
SCIENTIFIC NAME: *Portulaca oleracea*
STEMS: Prostrate, about 12" long.
LEAVES: Alternate, obovate or spatulate, up
to 1⅛" long.
FLOWERS: Solitary or clustered, yellow,
about ⅜" broad.
FRUIT: Very small capsules, splitting
around the middle.
HABITAT: Padre and Mustang Islands.
BLOOM PERIOD: Spring, summer, fall.

Chisme

FAMILY: Portulacaceae
SCIENTIFIC NAME: *Portulaca pilosa*
STEMS: Prostrate, about 6" long, woolly
around the leaf axils.
LEAVES: Alternate, linear, up to ⅝" long.
FLOWERS: Solitary or in clusters, purple,
about ½" broad, mixed with long soft
hairs.

FRUIT: Very small capsules, splitting
around the middle.
HABITAT: Various soils, throughout the
Texas beaches.
BLOOM PERIOD: Spring, summer, fall.
COMMENTS: Previously known as
Portulaca mundula.

Prostrate Chickweed

FAMILY: Caryophyllaceae
SCIENTIFIC NAME: *Stellaria prostrata*
STEMS: Prostrate or sprawling.
LEAVES: Opposite, the blades more or less triangular, up to 1¼" long.
FLOWERS: White, up to ⅜" broad.
FRUIT: A capsule, about ⅛" tall.
HABITAT: Padre and Mustang Islands, usually in moist places.
BLOOM PERIOD: Winter, spring, summer.

Blue Water Lily

FAMILY: Nymphaeaceae
SCIENTIFIC NAME: *Nymphaea elegans*
STEMS: None visible.
LEAVES: Blades more or less circular, green above and purple on the lower surface, up to 8" broad.
FLOWERS: Pale blue or violet, up to 6" broad.
FRUIT: Roundish, maturing under water.
HABITAT: Goose Island. Plants grow in water, the leaf blade usually floating on the surface.
BLOOM PERIOD: Spring, summer, fall.

Old Man's Beard

FAMILY: Ranunculaceae
SCIENTIFIC NAME: *Clematis drummondii*
STEMS: Hairy vines, stems up to 10' long.
LEAVES: Opposite, compound with 5 to 7
leaflets. Leaflets up to 1⅜" long.
FLOWERS: Radial, with 4 whitish sepals
about ½" long. Petals absent or
resembling stamens.
FRUIT: Achenes with white, feathery tails
up to 4" long.
HABITAT: Sandy soil, Padre Island.
BLOOM PERIOD: Spring, summer, fall.

Photographed at Lady Bird Johnson Wildflower Center, Austin, Texas

Agarita

FAMILY: Berberidaceae
SCIENTIFIC NAME: *Berberis trifoliolata*
STEMS: Evergreen shrubs up to 9' tall.
LEAVES: Compound with 3 prickly leaflets.
FLOWERS: Yellow, about ¼" broad, in small clusters.
FRUIT: Roundish red berries up to ⅜" broad.
HABITAT: Galveston Island.
BLOOM PERIOD: Late winter, spring.
COMMENTS: The berries are used to make jellies, pies, and beverages. The wood is used to make a yellow dye.

Also called *Berberis trifoliata*.

Carolina Snailseed

FAMILY: Menispermaceae
SCIENTIFIC NAME: *Cocculus carolinus*
STEMS: Twining vines up to 10' or longer.
LEAVES: Ovate or heart-shaped, 3½" or
longer.
FLOWERS: Greenish, about ⅛" broad, male
and female flowers on separate plants.
FRUIT: Red, juicy, ¼" broad or more, with
a single hard seed.
HABITAT: Sandy clay, Goose Island,
Galveston Island.
BLOOM PERIOD: Spring, summer.

Photograph by Scooter Cheatham

Sweetbay

FAMILY: Lauraceae
SCIENTIFIC NAME: *Persea borbonia*
STEMS: Evergreen shrubs or small trees up to 23' tall.
LEAVES: Alternate, elliptic, up to 8" long.
FLOWERS: Tiny, pale yellow, in clusters.
FRUIT: A blue or blue-black 1-seeded berry about ⅜" long.
HABITAT: In deep sands, often growing with oak. Padre and Goose Islands.
BLOOM PERIOD: Spring, early summer.
COMMENTS: The leaves are sometimes used in cooking as a substitute for the culinary bay leaf (*Laurus nobilis*), which is in the same plant family.

White Prickly Poppy

FAMILY: Papaveraceae

SCIENTIFIC NAME: *Argemone sanguinea*

STEMS: Erect, prickly, up to 39" tall, usually shorter.

LEAVES: Alternate, prickly, bleeding yellow sap when damaged.

FLOWERS: Radially symmetrical, usually white, sometimes purple, about 3" or more broad.

FRUIT: Very prickly capsules, about 2" tall.

HABITAT: Padre, Mustang, and Matagorda Islands.

BLOOM PERIOD: Spring, summer.

COMMENTS: Because of the prickly leaves and stems, the white prickly poppy is sometimes called a thistle. It is not related to the plant more commonly called a thistle.

Scrambled Eggs

FAMILY: Fumariaceae
SCIENTIFIC NAME: *Corydalis micrantha*
STEMS: Erect or falling over, up to 3' long.
LEAVES: Compound, the leaflets about ½"
long.
FLOWERS: Loosely arranged on the flower
stalk. Petals yellow, up to ½" or slightly
longer.
FRUIT: Capsules slender, straight or
curved, up to 1⅛" long.
HABITAT: Sandy soil, Padre and Mustang
Islands.
BLOOM PERIOD: Spring.

Photograph by Scooter Cheatham

Sea Rocket

FAMILY: Cruciferae

SCIENTIFIC NAME: *Cakile geniculata*

STEMS: Fleshy, branching, up to 20" tall.

LEAVES: Fleshy, up to 2¾" long, the margins smooth or with rounded teeth.

FLOWERS: White to lavender, about ¼" long. There are 4 petals.

FRUIT: Hardened, indehiscent, with a transverse partition. There is usually 1 seed in each of the 2 compartments.

HABITAT: In sands throughout the barrier islands.

BLOOM PERIOD: Spring, summer, fall.

COMMENTS: This plant is not showy, but it is one of the plants that seem to grow in pure sand. The fruit is unusual with its transverse partition. Generally the partition will be down the length of the fruit. The characteristic of the family is to have 4 petals rather than the more common 3, 5, or 6 petals.

Peppergrass

FAMILY: Cruciferae

SCIENTIFIC NAME: *Lepidium austrinum*

STEMS: Hairy, erect, branching, up to 24" tall, usually less.

LEAVES: Hairy, the basal leaves deeply cut, up to 3½" long. Upper leaves usually smooth or toothed.

FLOWERS: There are 4 tiny white petals ¹⁄₁₆" long or less.

FRUIT: Flattened, ovoid, up to ⅛" long.

HABITAT: Padre Island.

BLOOM PERIOD: Spring, summer.

COMMENTS: This is a plant that takes advantage of disturbed places. Its dry fruit are often mistaken for small leaves. *Lepidium virginicum* grows throughout the Texas coast. It is quite similar to *L. austrinum,* but it is hairless. *Lepidium lasiocarpum* occurs on Padre Island, and it is quite similar to *L. austrinum.* Its flower pedicels are markedly flattened, whereas those of *L. austrinum* are not.

Bladderpod

FAMILY: Cruciferae

SCIENTIFIC NAME: *Lesquerella lasiocarpa*

STEMS: Erect when young, sprawling when older, up to 24" long.

LEAVES: Hairy, mostly without petioles, deeply cut to toothed to smooth on the margins, up to 4" long.

FLOWERS: Yellow, with 4 petals about ⅜" long.

FRUIT: A flattened capsule, pointing downward.

HABITAT: Padre Island.

BLOOM PERIOD: Spring.

COMMENTS: There are two recognized varieties, var. *lasiocarpa* with two kinds of hairs on the capsule, and var. *berlandieri* with 1 kind of hair on the capsule.

A similar species, *L. grandiflora,* occurs on Padre and Mustang Islands. Its fruit do not point downward as do those of *L. lasiocarpa.*

Clammy Weed

FAMILY: Capparidaceae
SCIENTIFIC NAME: *Polanisia dodecandra*
subsp. *riograndensis*
STEMS: Erect, up to 2' tall.
LEAVES: Alternate, compound with 3
leaflets all originating at the same point.
Leaflets up to 2" long. Glands exude a
sticky, bad-smelling substance.
FLOWERS: Pink to purple, to about 1¼"
broad.
FRUIT: Capsules on short stalks, glandular.
HABITAT: Sand and sandy clay throughout
the Texas beaches and islands.
BLOOM PERIOD: Spring, summer, fall.
COMMENTS: *Polanisia erosa* has been
reported on Padre Island. It has narrower
leaflets, usually ⅛" or less broad.

Sundew

FAMILY: Droseraceae

SCIENTIFIC NAME: *Drosera annua*

STEMS: Very short, not noticeable.

LEAVES: Forming rosettes. Blades rounded to triangular, about ⅜" long and broad, with many glandular hairs producing a shiny, glutinous material at their apices.

FLOWERS: In erect bloom stalks with up to 6 flowers. Petals lavender-colored, about ⁵⁄₁₆" long.

FRUIT: An egg-shaped capsule about ⅛" long.

HABITAT: In damp sand, Padre Island, Goose Island.

BLOOM PERIOD: Spring.

COMMENTS: This is an insectivorous plant. The sticky hairs on the leaf blade catch an insect. Then the leaf curls over the insect and secretes digestive enzymes. The nutrients are then absorbed.

Also called *Drosera brevifolia*.

Photograph by Scooter Cheatham

Southern Dewberry

FAMILY: Rosaceae

SCIENTIFIC NAME: *Rubus trivialis*

STEMS: Woody, with very long canes that clamber over low plants. Stems and leaves armed with many curved prickles.

LEAVES: Alternate, compound with 3 leaflets. Leaflets up to 3" or longer.

FLOWERS: Resembling a rose with 5 sepals and 5 white petals, which are about ⅜" long.

FRUIT: Black when mature, sweet and juicy, up to ⅞" long.

HABITAT: Various soils, Padre and Matagorda Islands.

BLOOM PERIOD: Spring.

COMMENTS: Also known as *Rubus riograndis.*

Normal growth

Huisache

FAMILY: Leguminosae, subfamily Mimosoideae

SCIENTIFIC NAME: *Acacia farnesiana*

STEMS: Small trees up to 19' tall, with paired straight spines usually ⅜" long or less.

LEAVES: Alternate, compound, up to 3" or longer, usually with a gland near the middle of the petiole.

FLOWERS: Very small, in fragrant, orange-colored globose clusters about ⅜" broad.

FRUIT: Black, nearly cylindrical and curved, up to 3" long.

HABITAT: Throughout the Texas coast.

BLOOM PERIOD: Spring.

COMMENTS: Also known as *Acacia minuata*.

An unusual population of Huisache at Brazos Island and Boca Chica Beach grows prostrate, with spines about 2⅛" long.

General family characteristics are (1) alternate, compound leaves, and (2) the fruit is a legume (bean). This subfamily is sometimes classified as a family, and has tiny, radially symmetrical flowers, usually in globose or cylindrical clusters.

Prostrate form

Prairie Mimosa

FAMILY: Leguminosae, subfamily Mimosoideae
SCIENTIFIC NAME: *Desmanthus virgatus* var. *depressus*
STEMS: Sprawling or leaning, 30" long or more.
LEAVES: Alternate, compound, the leaflets up to ¼" long.
FLOWERS: Very small, white, in small clusters.
FRUIT: Legumes brown to reddish, flattened, straight or slightly curved, up to 2⅜" long.
HABITAT: Sandy soil, Padre Island.
BLOOM PERIOD: Spring, summer, fall.
COMMENTS: This species, unlike the others in this subfamily, does not have flowers clustered into tight globes or cylinders.

Powderpuff

FAMILY: Leguminosae, subfamily Mimosoideae
SCIENTIFIC NAME: *Mimosa strigillosa*
STEMS: Prostrate, 40" or longer.
LEAVES: Alternate, compound, up to 4¾" long.
FLOWERS: Very small, pink, in globose clusters up to ¾" broad.
FRUIT: Legumes flattened, jointed, up to ¾" long and ½" broad.
HABITAT: Sandy soils throughout the Texas beaches.
BLOOM PERIOD: Spring, summer.
COMMENTS: The leaves are sensitive, folding when touched.

Yellow Puff

FAMILY: Leguminosae, subfamily
Mimosoideae
SCIENTIFIC NAME: *Neptunia pubescens*
STEMS: Prostrate, up to 20" long.
LEAVES: Alternate, compound, up to 3½"
long.
FLOWERS: Very small, yellow, in globose
clusters about ½" broad.

FRUIT: Legumes brown or reddish,
flattened, about 1¼" long.
HABITAT: Sandy soil, throughout the Texas
beaches.
BLOOM PERIOD: Spring, summer, fall.
COMMENTS: The leaves are sensitive,
folding when touched.

Honey Mesquite

FAMILY: Leguminosae, subfamily
Mimosoideae
SCIENTIFIC NAME: *Prosopis glandulosa*
STEMS: Shrubs or trees up to 36' tall, with
sharp spines when young.
LEAVES: Alternate, compound, up to 6"
or longer.
FLOWERS: Very small, cream color, in
cylindrical clusters about 2" long.
FRUIT: Legumes brown or orange,
straight or curved, up to 8" long.
HABITAT: Sandy soil throughout the
Texas coast.
BLOOM PERIOD: Spring, summer.
COMMENTS: The beans are sweet and are
often eaten as candy by children.

Tornillo

FAMILY: Leguminosae, subfamily
Mimosoideae

SCIENTIFIC NAME: *Prosopis reptans* var.
cinerascens

STEMS: Small shrublets up to 18" tall,
sometimes taller, with sharp spines about
½" long.

LEAVES: Alternate, compound, up to ⅝"
long.

FLOWERS: Very small, orange-colored, in
globose clusters about ⅝" broad.

FRUIT: Legumes orange-colored, tightly
coiled to resemble the threads of a screw,
about 1½" long.

HABITAT: Clay or sandy clay, Brazos Island
and Boca Chica Beach.

BLOOM PERIOD: Spring, summer, fall.

COMMENTS: The identifying characteristic
of this shrublet is its fruit in the shape of a
screw.

Coiled bean

Sensitive Brier

FAMILY: Leguminosae, subfamily Mimosoideae

SCIENTIFIC NAME: *Schrankia latidens*

STEMS: Sprawling, about 40" or longer, with many curved prickles.

LEAVES: Alternate, compound, up to 2¾" long.

FLOWERS: Very small, pink, in globose clusters up to ¾" broad.

FRUIT: Legumes up to 2⅜" long, usually covered with prickles.

HABITAT: Sand dunes, Brazos, Padre, and Matagorda Islands.

BLOOM PERIOD: Spring, summer, fall.

COMMENTS: The leaves are sensitive, folding when touched.

Also known as *Mimosa latidens.*

Partridge Pea

FAMILY: Leguminosae, subfamily Caesalpinioideae

SCIENTIFIC NAME: *Chamaecrista fasciculata*

STEMS: Erect or leaning, reddish, up to 3' tall.

LEAVES: Alternate, compound, the leaflets up to ⅝" long, with glands on the petioles.

FLOWERS: Bilaterally symmetrical, in small clusters. Petals yellow, about ⅝" long.

FRUIT: Legumes brown or reddish, slightly curved, up to 2¾" long.

HABITAT: Sandy soils, throughout the Texas beaches.

BLOOM PERIOD: Spring, summer, fall.

COMMENTS: This subfamily of the Leguminosae has leaves that are alternate and compound, and the fruit is a legume (a bean). The flowers differ from those of the other two subfamilies in being somewhat bilaterally symmetrical.

Retama

FAMILY: Leguminosae, subfamily
Caesalpinioideae

SCIENTIFIC NAME: *Parkinsonia aculeata*

STEMS: Small trees up to 32' tall, with
sharp, curved spines about ⅜" long.

LEAVES: Alternate, compound, with broad
flattened rachises and short leaflets about
⅛" long.

FLOWERS: Bilaterally symmetrical, in
loose clusters. Petals yellow (1 of them
reddish), about ½" long.

FRUIT: Legumes brown, up to 4" long,
constricted between the seeds.

HABITAT: Padre and Matagorda Islands.

BLOOM PERIOD: Spring, summer.

COMMENTS: The leaflets tend to fall
during dry periods, leaving the bare,
flattened rachises.

Milkvetch

FAMILY: Leguminosae, subfamily
Papilionoideae

SCIENTIFIC NAME: *Astragalus nuttallianus*

STEMS: Prostrate or weakly leaning, up to
12" or longer.

LEAVES: Alternate, compound, the leaflets
up to ⅝" long.

FLOWERS: Markedly bilateral, several per
raceme. Petals purplish or white, ¼"–⅜"
long.

FRUIT: Legumes small, up to ¾" long,
curved near the base.

HABITAT: Sandy areas, Padre Island.

BLOOM PERIOD: Spring.

COMMENTS: Several varieties are
recognized.

This subfamily of the Leguminosae is
characterized by markedly bilateral
flowers and once-compound (rarely
simple) leaves.

Plains Wild Indigo

FAMILY: Leguminosae, subfamily Papilionoideae

SCIENTIFIC NAME: *Baptisia leucophaea*

STEMS: Erect perennials up to 32" tall.

LEAVES: Alternate, compound with 3 leaflets, each up to 2¼" long and 1⅛" broad.

FLOWERS: In more or less pendulous clusters, light yellow, up to ⅞" long.

FRUIT: Legumes dark brown or black, inflated, up to 2" long and 1" broad, with a slender tip.

HABITAT: Sand dunes, Boca Chica Beach, Padre, Brazos, and Matagorda Islands.

BLOOM PERIOD: Spring.

COMMENTS: The leaf petioles are very short or absent, giving the appearance of 3 simple leaves instead of 1 compound leaf. After the plant dies, the leaves turn a silver color.

Also known as *Baptisia bracteata* var. *laevicaulis*.

Butterfly Pea

FAMILY: Leguminosae, subfamily Papilionoideae
SCIENTIFIC NAME: *Centrosema virginianum*
STEMS: Twining or trailing vines, up to 4' long.
LEAVES: Alternate, compound with 3 leaflets, each up to 2¼" long.
FLOWERS: Usually solitary, purple to pale lavender, up to 1⅛" long.
FRUIT: Legumes up to 4¾" long and ¼" or less broad.
HABITAT: Sandy soil, throughout the Texas coast.
BLOOM PERIOD: Spring, summer.

Crotolaria

FAMILY: Leguminosae, subfamily Papilionoideae
SCIENTIFIC NAME: *Crotolaria retusa*
STEMS: Erect, up to 3' tall.
LEAVES: Alternate, simple, up to 3⅛" long and ⅝"–¾" broad.
FLOWERS: Yellow, often with some reddish coloring, up to 1½" long and about 1" broad.
FRUIT: Legumes cylindrical, many-seeded, up to 1¾" or more in length.
HABITAT: Sandy soil, Padre Island.
BLOOM PERIOD: Fall.
COMMENTS: This species is considered an escape from cultivation.
    Crotolaria incana and *C. sagittalis* also grow on our beaches and islands. *C. incana* has 3-foliate compound leaves. *C. sagittalis* has simple leaves ⅝" or narrower, while *C. retusa* has simple leaves ¾" or broader.

Dalea

FAMILY: Leguminosae, subfamily Papilionoideae

SCIENTIFIC NAME: *Dalea emarginata*

STEMS: Erect to leaning and falling over, up to 20" long.

LEAVES: Alternate, compound, with 13–17 leaflets, each up to ⅜" long.

FLOWERS: Purple, about ³⁄₁₆" long.

FRUIT: Legumes small, hairy, with 1 or 2 seeds.

HABITAT: Sand dunes and clay soils, throughout the Texas beaches.

BLOOM PERIOD: Spring, summer, fall.

COMMENTS: The genus *Dalea* is characterized by the presence of yellowish glands on the lower surfaces of the leaves and calyxes.

Dalea pogonathera, D. lanata, and *D. obovata* also grow on the Texas beaches. *D. pogonathera,* like *D. emarginata,* is hairless. It has 7 or fewer leaflets per leaf, and *D. emarginata* has 13 or more leaflets per leaf. The other two species are both hairy. *D. obovata* has 5 stamens, and *D. lanata* has more numerous stamens.

Woolly Dalea

FAMILY: Leguminosae, subfamily
Papilionoideae
SCIENTIFIC NAME: *Dalea lanata*
STEMS: Prostrate, very hairy, up to 24"
long.
LEAVES: Alternate, compound with 9–13
leaflets, very hairy, the leaflets up to ³⁄₁₆"
long.
FLOWERS: Purple, about ¼" long.
FRUIT: Legumes small and hairy, with 1 or
2 seeds.
HABITAT: Loose sand, Brazos and Padre
Islands and Boca Chica Beach.
BLOOM PERIOD: Summer, fall.
COMMENTS: The glands on the lower
surfaces of the leaflets are generally
hidden by the abundant hairs.

Bearded Dalea

FAMILY: Leguminosae, subfamily
Papilionideae
SCIENTIFIC NAME: *Dalea pogonathera*
STEMS: Weak, erect to falling over.
LEAVES: Alternate, compound, with 5–7
leaflets, about ³⁄₈" long.
FLOWERS: Purple, about ³⁄₁₆" long.
FRUIT: A small, hairy legume.
HABITAT: Sand or sandy clay, Padre Island.
BLOOM PERIOD: Winter, spring, summer.
COMMENTS: The flowers on this species
are larger and more noticeable than those
of the other three species.

Coral Bean

FAMILY: Leguminosae, subfamily Papilionoideae
SCIENTIFIC NAME: *Erythrina herbacea*
STEMS: Thorny shrubs up to 6½' tall.
LEAVES: Alternate, compound with 3 leaflets. Leaflets up to 2¾" long.
FLOWERS: Red, up to 2" long.
FRUIT: Legumes 3"–8" long, with bright red seeds.
HABITAT: Sandy soil, Padre, Mustang, and Matagorda Islands.
BLOOM PERIOD: Spring.
COMMENTS: This species is often cultivated.

Scarlet Pea

FAMILY: Leguminosae, subfamily Papilionoideae
SCIENTIFIC NAME: *Indigofera miniata*
STEMS: Prostrate, hairy, about 40" long.
LEAVES: Alternate, compound, and hairy. Leaflets up to 1" long.
FLOWERS: Salmon or brick-red color, up to ¾" long.
FRUIT: Legumes up to 1⅛" long.
HABITAT: Sandy soils, throughout the Texas beaches.
BLOOM PERIOD: Spring, summer, fall.

Purple Bean

FAMILY: Leguminosae, subfamily
Papilionoideae
SCIENTIFIC NAME: *Macroptilium
atropurpureum*
STEMS: Twining, herbaceous vines, often
hairy.
LEAVES: Alternate, compound, with 3
leaflets. Leaflets up to 2" long.
FLOWERS: Variable in color, the darkest
ones deep purple, appearing black. The
petals are up to ¾" long.
FRUIT: Legumes nearly straight, up to
3⅛" long.
HABITAT: Sandy soils, Brazos and Padre
Islands.
BLOOM PERIOD: Spring.
COMMENTS: Formerly known as *Phaseolus
atropurpureus.*

Bur Clover

FAMILY: Leguminosae, subfamily
Papilionoideae
SCIENTIFIC NAME: *Medicago polymorpha*
STEMS: Leaning or sprawling, up to 18"
long.
LEAVES: Alternate, compound, the leaflets
about ¾" long.
FLOWERS: Yellow, about ⅛" long.
FRUIT: Legumes coiled and prickly, about
¼" broad.
HABITAT: Open or disturbed places, Padre
and Matagorda Islands.
BLOOM PERIOD: Spring.
COMMENTS: The coiled, prickly legumes
make this species easily recognized.

White Sweet Clover

FAMILY: Leguminosae, subfamily Papilionoideae

SCIENTIFIC NAME: *Melilotus albus*

STEMS: Erect, up to 40" tall.

LEAVES: Alternate, compound, with 3 leaflets. Leaflets up to ¾" long.

FLOWERS: White, about ¼" long.

FRUIT: Legumes ovoid or globose, usually 1-seeded.

HABITAT: Open places, Padre Island.

BLOOM PERIOD: Spring, summer.

COMMENTS: Native to the Old World, introduced and naturalized here.

Sour Clover

FAMILY: Leguminosae, subfamily
Papilionoideae
SCIENTIFIC NAME: *Melilotus indicus*
STEMS: Erect, up to 18" or taller.
LEAVES: Alternate, compound, with 3
leaflets. Leaflets up to ¾" long.
FLOWERS: Yellow, about ⅛" long.
FRUIT: Legumes flattened, more or less
circular in outline, usually 1-seeded.
HABITAT: Sandy clay, Padre, Mustang, and
Matagorda Islands.
BLOOM PERIOD: Spring, summer.
COMMENTS: Native to the Mediterranean
area, introduced and naturalized here.

Snoutbean

FAMILY: Leguminosae, subfamily
Papilionoideae
SCIENTIFIC NAME: *Rhynchosia americana*
STEMS: Twining or trailing vines.
LEAVES: Alternate, simple, heart-shaped or
kidney-shaped, up to 1⅛" long and 1½"
broad.
FLOWERS: Yellow, up to ⅜" long.
FRUIT: Legumes flattened, usually with 1
or 2 seeds, up to ¾" long. The two halves
twist as the legume splits open.
HABITAT: Sandy soil, throughout the Texas
beaches.
BLOOM PERIOD: Spring, summer, fall.
COMMENTS: This is one of the rare
members of the Leguminosae with simple
leaves. However, it has the typical flower
and fruit of the family.

Least Snoutbean

FAMILY: Leguminosae, subfamily
Papilionoideae

SCIENTIFIC NAME: *Rhynchosia minima*

STEMS: Twining or trailing vines.

LEAVES: Alternate, compound with 3
leaflets. Leaflets lance-shaped, up to 1⅛"
long.

FLOWERS: Yellow, up to ¼" long.

FRUIT: Legumes flattened, curved, ½" or
slightly longer. The two halves twist as the
legume splits open.

HABITAT: Sand or sandy clay, Brazos,
Padre, and Mustang Islands.

BLOOM PERIOD: Spring, summer, fall.

COMMENTS: *Rhynchosia minima,* with
3-foliate, compound leaves, is easily
distinguished from *R. americana,* which
has simple leaves. Two other species are
found on Texas beaches. *R. reniformis*
usually has simple kidney-shaped or oval
leaves, and the stems do not twine.
R. senna has only 1–3 flowers emerging
from the leaf axil.

Rattlebush

FAMILY: Leguminosae, subfamily
Papilionoideae

SCIENTIFIC NAME: *Sesbania drummondii*

STEMS: Woody shrubs 4'–10' tall.

LEAVES: Compound, the leaflets about
1⅜" long.

FLOWERS: Yellow, pea-shaped, up to ⅝"
long, in pendulous clusters.

FRUIT: Legumes about 2⅜" long, with 4
ridges along the full length.

HABITAT: Goose, Padre, Matagorda, and
Galveston Islands; Bolivar Peninsula.

BLOOM PERIOD: Late spring to fall.

COMMENTS: Four species of *Sesbania* are
reported for the Texas coast. *S. drummondii*
and *S. punicea* have legumes with 4 ridges
running down the full length;
S. drummondii has yellow corollas and
S. punicea has orange- to rose-colored
corollas. *S. macrocarpa* has yellow corollas
that are ⁷⁄₁₆"–⅝" long; *S. vesicaria* has
yellowish corollas, sometimes tinged with
pink, and they are less than ⅜" long.

Coffee Bean

FAMILY: Leguminosae, subfamily
Papilionoideae

SCIENTIFIC NAME: *Sesbania macrocarpa*

STEMS: Annuals, sometimes woody, up to
13' tall.

LEAVES: Alternate, compound, the leaflets
up to ⅞" or longer.

FLOWERS: Yellow, sometimes with red
lines, up to ⅝" long.

FRUIT: Legumes linear, up to 6¾" long.

HABITAT: Padre, Mustang, and Matagorda
Islands.

BLOOM PERIOD: Summer, fall.

COMMENTS: Also known as *Sesbania
exaltata*.

Yellow Sophora

FAMILY: Leguminosae, subfamily
Papilionoideae
SCIENTIFIC NAME: *Sophora tomentosa* var.
occidentalis
STEMS: Shrubs up to 6½' tall.
LEAVES: Alternate, compound, densely
hairy. Leaflets up to 1¾" long.
FLOWERS: Yellow, up to ⅞" long.
FRUIT: Legumes linear, up to 5½" long,
constricted between the seeds.
HABITAT: Sandy soil, Boca Chica Beach,
Brazos, Padre, and Mustang Islands.
BLOOM PERIOD: Spring, summer, fall.

Trailing Wild Bean

FAMILY: Leguminosae, subfamily Papilionoideae

SCIENTIFIC NAME: *Strophostyles helvula*

STEMS: Twining or trailing vines.

LEAVES: Alternate, compound with 3 leaflets.

FLOWERS: Cream color, aging to lavender, up to ⅜" long.

FRUIT: Legumes linear and slightly flattened, with several seeds.

HABITAT: Sandy soil, Padre Island, Bolivar Peninsula.

BLOOM PERIOD: Spring, summer, fall.

Vetch

FAMILY: Leguminosae, subfamily Papilionoideae

SCIENTIFIC NAME: *Vicia ludoviciana* var. *texana*

STEMS: Herbaceous vines with stems 24" or longer.

LEAVES: Alternate, compound, with a tendril at the tip. The leaflets are up to ⅝" long.

FLOWERS: Blue, up to ¼" or longer.

FRUIT: Legumes flattened, up to ¾" long.

HABITAT: Padre, Mustang, and Matagorda Islands.

BLOOM PERIOD: Spring.

COMMENTS: The tendril at the tip of the leaf identifies this vine.

Also called *Vicia ludoviciana* subsp. *ludoviciana*.

Wild Cowpea

FAMILY: Leguminosae, subfamily Papilionoideae

SCIENTIFIC NAME: *Vigna luteola*

STEMS: Twining vines with stems 6' or longer.

LEAVES: Alternate, compound with 3 leaflets. Leaflets up to 2¾" long.

FLOWERS: Yellow, up to ¾" long.

FRUIT: Legumes flattened, up to 2" long.

HABITAT: Sandy soils, Padre, Galveston Islands.

BLOOM PERIOD: All seasons.

Carolina Wild Geranium

FAMILY: Geraniaceae
SCIENTIFIC NAME: *Geranium carolinianum*
STEMS: Leaning or falling over, about 20" long.
LEAVES: Lobed, about 1"–2¼" broad.
FLOWERS: About ¼" broad, pink to lavender, in clusters.
FRUIT: Dry, 1-seeded, with a straight projection about ½" long.
HABITAT: Sandy soils, Galveston Island.
BLOOM PERIOD: Spring.

Drummond Oxalis

FAMILY: Oxalidaceae
SCIENTIFIC NAME: *Oxalis drummondii*
STEMS: None.
LEAVES: Compound with 3 leaflets.
Leaflets usually shaped like a boomerang,
or V-shaped, up to 2" broad.
FLOWERS: Radially symmetrical, purple,
occasionally white, up to ¾" long.
FRUIT: Capsules up to ⅜" long.
HABITAT: Various soils, Padre, Mustang,
and Matagorda Islands.
BLOOM PERIOD: Spring, summer, fall.

Wood Sorrel

FAMILY: Oxalidaceae
SCIENTIFIC NAME: *Oxalis stricta*
STEMS: Erect or falling over, up to 16"
long.
LEAVES: Compound with 3 leaflets.
Leaflets obcordate, up to ¾" long.
FLOWERS: Radially symmetrical, bright
yellow, ⅜"–½" broad.
FRUIT: Capsules up to 1¼" long.
HABITAT: Padre, Mustang, and Matagorda
Islands.
BLOOM PERIOD: Spring, summer.
COMMENTS: This species has previously
been called *Oxalis dillenii.*

Flax

FAMILY: Linaceae
SCIENTIFIC NAME: *Linum alatum*
STEMS: Erect, up to 16" tall.
LEAVES: Opposite on lower parts, alternate higher up. Blades linear, up to ¾" long.
FLOWERS: Yellow with reddish basal lines. Petals 5, about ¾" long.
FRUIT: A capsule, ¼" tall or less.
HABITAT: Sandy soils, Boca Chica Beach; Brazos, Padre, Mustang, and Matagorda Islands.
BLOOM PERIOD: Spring, summer, fall.
COMMENTS: *Linum rigidum* also is reported on our beaches. It has sepals with fine, regular teeth, while *L. alatum* has sepals with coarse, irregular teeth. The flowers of the two species are similar.

Photograph by Scooter Cheatham

Goat Head

FAMILY: Zygophyllaceae

SCIENTIFIC NAME: *Tribulus terrestris*

STEMS: Prostrate, 20" or longer.

LEAVES: Compound, the leaflets about ⅝"
long.

FLOWERS: Yellow, from the leaf axils,
about ⅝" broad.

FRUIT: About ⅝" broad with large spines.

HABITAT: Sandy soils, Padre and Mustang
Islands.

BLOOM PERIOD: Spring, summer, fall.

Hercules' Club

FAMILY: Rutaceae

SCIENTIFIC NAME: *Zanthoxylum clava-herculis*

STEMS: Shrubs or small trees up to 16' or taller, with many prickles resembling those of a rose bush.

LEAVES: Alternate, pinnately compound, prickly, the leaflets up to 3⅛" long.

FLOWERS: Very small, in large terminal clusters, unisexual, male and female flowers on separate plants. Petals yellowish.

FRUIT: Small, dry, and falling apart when mature.

HABITAT: Sand, sandy clay. Padre, Goose, and Galveston Islands.

BLOOM PERIOD: Spring.

COMMENTS: *Zanthoxylum clava-herculis,* with its greater size, larger prickles and showy flowers, is easily distinguished from *Z. fagara.* The leaves have a citrus odor when bruised.

Lime Pricklyash

FAMILY: Rutaceae
SCIENTIFIC NAME: *Zanthoxylum fagara*
STEMS: Erect shrubs up to 10' tall, with cat-claw-like prickles.
LEAVES: Alternate, compound, the leaflets about 1" long.
FLOWERS: Very tiny, unisexual, seen only with careful examination.
FRUIT: Roundish, about ⅛" broad, splitting open about half the length.
HABITAT: Various soils, Padre and Matagorda Islands.
BLOOM PERIOD: Spring.
COMMENTS: The leaves give off a citrus odor when bruised.

Chinaberry

FAMILY: Meliaceae
SCIENTIFIC NAME: *Melia azedarach*
STEMS: Trees up to 48' tall, the crowns rounded and umbrella-like.
LEAVES: Alternate, compound, up to 14" long. Leaflets toothed, 2"–2¼" long.
FLOWERS: In slender, open clusters. Flowers fragrant, lavender with dark purple centers, about ⅜" long.
FRUIT: A 1-seeded, juicy roundish fruit, ⅜"–⅝" broad, yellow when mature.
HABITAT: Mustang, Matagorda, and Galveston Islands.
BLOOM PERIOD: Spring.
COMMENTS: This tree is a native to Asia, escaped from cultivation.

White Milkwort

FAMILY: Polygalaceae
SCIENTIFIC NAME: *Polygala alba*
STEMS: Erect, up to 12" tall.
LEAVES: Alternate, sometimes whorled basally. Blades linear, up to ¾" long.
FLOWERS: Tiny, white, densely clustered.
FRUIT: A tiny capsule.
HABITAT: Sandy soil, Boca Chica Beach, Brazos and Padre Islands.
BLOOM PERIOD: Spring, summer, fall.

Cardinal Feather

FAMILY: Euphorbiaceae
SCIENTIFIC NAME: *Acalypha radians*
STEMS: Sprawling, hairy, up to 16" long.
LEAVES: Hairy, blades more or less rounded, up to ⅜" long. Margins deeply lobed.
FLOWERS: Tiny, unisexual, the sexes on separate plants. Both sexes have reddish flowers. The female flowers have prominent red styles.

FRUIT: A tiny 3-seeded capsule.
HABITAT: Sandy soil, Boca Chica Beach, Brazos and Padre Islands.
BLOOM PERIOD: Spring, fall.
COMMENTS: Although the individual flowers are tiny, the clusters of flowers, especially the female ones, are easily seen.

Female

Male

Bull Nettle

FAMILY: Euphorbiaceae

SCIENTIFIC NAME: *Cnidoscolus texanus*

STEMS: Erect, up to 32" tall, covered with stinging hairs.

LEAVES: Palmately lobed, up to 6" broad, covered with stinging hairs.

FLOWERS: White, up to 1⅛" broad, in clusters, with male and female flowers on the same inflorescence. The female flowers are somewhat smaller.

FRUIT: A 3-lobed capsule about 1" long. Each compartment holds 1 seed.

HABITAT: Dunes and sandy clay, Padre and Mustang Islands.

BLOOM PERIOD: Spring, summer, fall.

COMMENTS: If this plant is touched, the stinging hairs inject a painful substance under the skin. The sepals make up the colorful part of the flower. There are no petals. The seeds are thrown away from the parent plant when the capsule pops open.

Woolly Croton

FAMILY: Euphorbiaceae

SCIENTIFIC NAME: *Croton capitatus* var. *lindheimeri*

STEMS: Erect, up to 40" tall.

LEAVES: Blades ovate, up to 3" long and 1½" broad, covered with star-shaped hairs.

FLOWERS: Very small, with male and female flowers on the same inflorescence.

FRUIT: A 3-lobed, 3-seeded capsule up to ⅜" long.

HABITAT: Sandy soils, throughout the Texas beaches.

BLOOM PERIOD: Spring, summer, fall.

COMMENTS: Seven species of *Croton* are reported growing on the Texas coast. They can be distinguished with the following key:

1. 1 seed per capsule. . . . *C. monanthogynus*

1'. 3 seeds per capsule . . . . (2)

2. Leaves toothed . . . .*C. glandulosus*

2'. Leaves not toothed . . . . (3)

3. Tiny brown dots and brown veins on the lower surfaces of the leaves . . . . *C. punctatus*

3'. Leaves not as above . . . . (4)

4. Male and female flowers on separate plants . . . .*C. parksii*

4'. Male and female flowers on the same plant . . . . (5)

5. Stems and leaves scaly, lower surfaces of leaves silvery . . . . *C. argyranthemus*

5'. Plants not as above . . . . (6)

6. Corollas hairy . . . .*C. capitatus*

6'. Corollas with silvery scales on the lower surfaces . . . .*C. coryi*

Bristly Croton

FAMILY: Euphorbiaceae

SCIENTIFIC NAME: *Croton glandulosus* var. *pubentissimus*

STEMS: Erect, up to 22" tall.

LEAVES: Blades ovate, up to 2⅝" long and 1" broad, covered with star-shaped hairs. The margins are toothed.

FLOWERS: Very small, with male and female flowers on the same inflorescence.

FRUIT: A 3-lobed, 3-seeded capsule up to ¼" long.

HABITAT: Sandy soils throughout the Texas beaches.

BLOOM PERIOD: All seasons.

COMMENTS: For distinguishing the different *Croton* species, refer to Comments under *C. capitatus* var. *lindheimeri*.

Beach Tea

FAMILY: Euphorbiaceae

SCIENTIFIC NAME: *Croton punctatus*

STEMS: Erect, up to 28" tall.

LEAVES: Blades mostly ovate, up to 2⅜" long and 1½" broad, with star-shaped hairs and scales. On the lower surfaces are tiny spots and often brown veins.

FLOWERS: Very small, with male and female flowers usually on separate plants.

FRUIT: A 3-lobed capsule about ¼" long.

HABITAT: Sandy soils, throughout the Texas beaches.

BLOOM PERIOD: Spring, summer, fall.

COMMENTS: For distinguishing the different *Croton* species, refer to Comments under *C. capitatus* var. *lindheimeri*.

Undersurface of leaf, showing glands

Spurge

FAMILY: Euphorbiaceae
SCIENTIFIC NAME: *Euphorbia cordifolia*
STEMS: Prostrate, up to 20" long, bleeding milky juice if broken.
LEAVES: Opposite, the blades elliptic, up to ⅜" long and ¼" broad, bleeding milky juice if broken.
FLOWERS: Very tiny, but with 4 white or pinkish glandular appendages about ¹⁄₁₆" long.
FRUIT: A 3-lobed capsule about ¹⁄₁₆" long.
HABITAT: Sand dunes, Brazos Island and Boca Chica Beach.
BLOOM PERIOD: Spring, summer.
COMMENTS: Nine species of *Euphorbia* are reported growing on the beaches and islands: *E. ammannioides* (not pictured), *E. cordifolia, E. corollata* (not pictured), *E. heterophylla, E. hypericifolia* (not pictured), *E. innocua* (not pictured), *E. maculata* (not pictured), *E. nutans,* and *E. serpens* (not pictured). Most of them are difficult to distinguish without a microscope or a strong hand lens, and for some of them, pictures would not be useful for identification.

Wild Poinsettia, Catalina

FAMILY: Euphorbiaceae
SCIENTIFIC NAME: *Euphorbia heterophylla*
STEMS: Erect, up to 32" or taller.
LEAVES: Opposite on low part of stem, alternate above. Blades mostly ovate, up to 4" long, the margins usually toothed. When plants bloom, the upper leaves have bright pinkish markings.
FLOWERS: Very tiny, in apical clusters.
FRUIT: A 3-lobed capsule about ⅛" tall.
HABITAT: Sandy soil, Goose Island.
BLOOM PERIOD: Spring, summer, fall.
COMMENTS: Formerly called *Poinsettia heterophylla*.

Eyebane

FAMILY: Euphorbiaceae

SCIENTIFIC NAME: *Euphorbia nutans*

STEMS: Erect, up to 20" tall.

LEAVES: Opposite, the blades oblanceolate, often slightly curved, up to 1⅛" long and ¼" broad. The margins are toothed.

FLOWERS: Very tiny, with 4 white glandular appendages about ¹⁄₁₆" long.

FRUIT: A 3-lobed capsule a little over ¹⁄₁₆" tall.

HABITAT: Brazos Island, Boca Chica Beach.

BLOOM PERIOD: Spring, summer, fall.

COMMENTS: *Euphorbia hypericifolia* and *E. nutans* are similar in growth habit, but the capsules of *E. nutans* are over ¹⁄₁₆" tall, while those of *E. hypericifolia* are less than ¹⁄₁₆" tall.

Leaf Flower

FAMILY: Euphorbiaceae
SCIENTIFIC NAME: *Phyllanthus polygonoides*
STEMS: Herbaceous, up to 16" tall.
LEAVES: Alternate, the blades elliptic to
spatulate, up to ½" long and ³⁄₁₆" broad.
FLOWERS: Male and female flowers
usually on the same plant, up to ⅛" broad,
usually in the axils of the leaves.
FRUIT: A tiny 3-compartmented capsule.
HABITAT: Sandy clay, Padre and
Matagorda Islands.
BLOOM PERIOD: All seasons.
COMMENTS: *P. abnormis* and *P. pudens* also
grow on the Texas beaches. For
identification, the species must be
carefully examined with a high-powered
lens or a microscope.

Poison Ivy

FAMILY: Anacardiaceae

SCIENTIFIC NAME: *Toxicodendron radicans*

STEMS: Deciduous vines, occasionally low shrubs.

LEAVES: Compound, almost always with 3 leaflets. The terminal leaflet grows up to 8" long, usually less. The midvein of the lateral leaflets divides them into unequal "halves."

FLOWERS: In clusters of very small flowers, mixed unisexual and bisexual.

FRUIT: A drupe, cream-colored, roundish, about ¼" broad.

HABITAT: Sandy soil, Galveston Island.

BLOOM PERIOD: Spring.

COMMENTS: Poison ivy is familiar to almost everyone. Contact with the plant can cause a painful rash. Some are so sensitive that they are affected by the volatile compounds near the plant, developing a rash without actually touching it. Sometimes the leaves turn an attractive reddish color in the fall, but it is not recommended that they be collected for floral arrangements.

Also known as *Rhus toxicodendron*.

Yaupon

FAMILY: Aquifoliaceae

SCIENTIFIC NAME: *Ilex vomitoria*

STEMS: Evergreen shrubs up to 10',
sometimes taller.

LEAVES: Tough, dark green above, elliptic,
up to 2¼" long.

FLOWERS: In clusters in the leaf axils.
Petals white, about ⅛" long.

FRUIT: Rounded, bright red berries
(technically called drupes), about ¼" in
diameter.

HABITAT: Sandy soils, Goose, Matagorda,
and Galveston Islands.

BLOOM PERIOD: Spring.

COMMENTS: This shrub is often cultivated
for its red berries. It is in the same genus
as the well-known Christmas holly.

Serjania

FAMILY: Sapindaceae
SCIENTIFIC NAME: *Serjania brachycarpa*
STEMS: Vines with tendrils.
LEAVES: Compound. Leaflets ovate, up to
1⅜" long, the margins toothed.
FLOWERS: Whitish or greenish, about ¼"
broad.
FRUIT: Dry, about ½" long, breaking apart
into 3 winged seeds.
HABITAT: Goose Island.
BLOOM PERIOD: Summer, fall.

Brasil

FAMILY: Rhamnaceae
SCIENTIFIC NAME: *Condalia hookeri*
STEMS: Thorny shrubs or small trees up to
13' or taller.
LEAVES: Alternate, the blades obovate or
spatulate, up to 1" long.
FLOWERS: Very insignificant, solitary or in
clusters.
FRUIT: 1-seeded with a thin juicy outer
part, ¼" or more broad. Black when
mature.
HABITAT: Goose Island, Matagorda Island.
BLOOM PERIOD: Spring, summer.

Peppervine

FAMILY: Vitaceae
SCIENTIFIC NAME: *Ampelopsis arborea*
STEMS: Woody vines.
LEAVES: Alternate, compound, the leaflets up to 2" long.
FLOWERS: Very tiny, greenish, in clusters.
FRUIT: Black when ripe, about ¼" broad, in clusters resembling a bunch of grapes.
HABITAT: Sandy soil, Galveston Island.
BLOOM PERIOD: Spring to summer.

Marine Ivy

FAMILY: Vitaceae
SCIENTIFIC NAME: *Cissus incisa*
STEMS: Woody vines with tendrils.
LEAVES: Alternate, succulent or fleshy, malodorous when bruised. Blades simple to deeply lobed or compound, up to 2⅜" broad.
FLOWERS: Very tiny, greenish.
FRUIT: Berries up to ⅜" long, in clusters resembling a bunch of grapes, turning black when mature.
HABITAT: Climbing on trees, shrubs, and fences, Padre, Mustang, Goose, Matagorda, and Galveston Islands.
BLOOM PERIOD: Spring, summer.
COMMENTS: This species is in the same family as the commercial grape.

Virginia Creeper

FAMILY: Vitaceae

SCIENTIFIC NAME: *Parthenocissus quinquefolia*

STEMS: Woody vines with tendrils.

LEAVES: Alternate, palmate, with usually 5 leaflets, the leaflets up to 6" long.

FLOWERS: Greenish, clustered, less than ⅛" broad.

FRUIT: Berries about 3⁄16" broad, blue-black when mature, in clusters resembling a bunch of grapes.

HABITAT: Climbing on trees, shrubs, and fences, Goose Island.

BLOOM PERIOD: Spring, summer.

COMMENTS: The specific epithet *quinquefolia* refers to the 5 leaflets that are usually present on each leaf.

Mustang Grape

FAMILY: Vitaceae

SCIENTIFIC NAME: *Vitis mustangensis*

STEMS: Woody vines with tendrils.

LEAVES: Alternate, palmately lobed, up to 7½" broad.

FLOWERS: Very tiny, greenish.

FRUIT: Purple to black berries ½"–⅝" broad, in clusters.

HABITAT: Sandy soil, edge of woods, Goose Island.

BLOOM PERIOD: Spring.

COMMENTS: The vines are sometimes cultivated and a very desirable jelly is made from the grapes.

Wine Cup, Poppy Mallow

FAMILY: Malvaceae
SCIENTIFIC NAME: *Callirhoë involucrata*
STEMS: Mostly creeping, around 40" long.
LEAVES: Alternate, the blades deeply cut, ovate in outline, up to 1" long and 1⅛" broad.
FLOWERS: Solitary from the leaf axils, the petals reddish purple, up to 1" long.
FRUIT: A flattened capsule ¼"–⅜" broad, breaking apart into separate segments each with 1 seed.
HABITAT: Sandy clay, Padre and Mustang Islands.
BLOOM PERIOD: Spring.
COMMENTS: The Malvaceae family is easy to recognize. It has 5 sepals and 5 petals, and (the major characteristic) the stamen filaments grow together to form a tube around the style, giving the appearance of many stamens emerging from the style.

Malva Loca

FAMILY: Malvaceae

SCIENTIFIC NAME: *Malvastrum americanum*

STEMS: Erect, up to 30" tall.

LEAVES: Alternate, the blades ovate, up to 2½" long.

FLOWERS: In dense terminal cylindrical clusters. Petals orange-yellow, about ¼" long.

FRUIT: A capsule breaking apart into 1-seeded segments.

HABITAT: Variable, Padre and Matagorda Islands.

BLOOM PERIOD: All seasons.

Three-Lobe False Mallow

FAMILY: Malvaceae
SCIENTIFIC NAME: *Malvastrum coromandelianum*
STEMS: Erect, up to 39" tall, usually much shorter.
LEAVES: Alternate, the blades ovate, toothed, up to 2¼" long.
FLOWERS: Usually solitary, yellow to orange, ½"–⅝" broad.
FRUIT: A barbed capsule dividing into individual segments, each with 1 seed.
HABITAT: Disturbed places, Padre and Galveston Islands.
BLOOM PERIOD: All seasons.

Turk's-Cap Mallow

FAMILY: Malvaceae
SCIENTIFIC NAME: *Malvaviscus arboreus* var. *drummondii*
STEMS: Erect, up to 10' tall in cultivation. Wild plants are usually much shorter.
LEAVES: Alternate, the blades roundish or heart-shaped, up to 3½" long and broad.
FLOWERS: Usually solitary from the leaf axils. Petals red, up to 1½" long, remaining closed around the style.
FRUIT: Red, juicy, said to be edible.
HABITAT: Variable, Padre and Matagorda Islands.
BLOOM PERIOD: Spring, summer, fall.
COMMENTS: The cultivated variety is a bigger plant. The flowers are also bigger and are produced in greater quantities.

Also known as *Malvaviscus drummondii*.

Bracted Sida

FAMILY: Malvaceae
SCIENTIFIC NAME: *Sida ciliaris*
STEMS: Prostrate or leaning, up to 12"
long.
LEAVES: Alternate, the blades heart-
shaped, up to 2¾" long.
FLOWERS: In small tight apical clusters.
Petals yellow to purple, up to ⅝" long.
FRUIT: Dry, splitting either partially or
not at all.
HABITAT: Various, Padre and Matagorda
Islands.
BLOOM PERIOD: Spring, summer, fall.
COMMENTS: Six species of Sida have been
reported for the Texas coast. The
following key can be used to distinguish
them.

1. Plants velvety with soft hairs
.... *S. cordifolia*

1'. Plants not velvety. .... (2)

2. Flowers salmon to rose-colored,
mostly in tight clusters enclosed
in bracts. .... *S. ciliaris*

2'. Flowers yellow to orange, not
enclosed in bracts .... (3)

3. Petioles of largest leaves with a
spinelike protuberance ...... *S. spinosa*

3'. Petioles without spinelike
protuberances .... (4)

4. Flower petals ½"–1¹⁄₁₆" long
.... *S. lindheimeri*

4'. Flower petals ⁷⁄₁₆" or less long ...... (5)

5. Leaf blades rounded
or heart-shaped basally ..... *S. abutifolia*

5'. Leaf blades mostly tapering
to the base .... *S. rhombifolia*

Sida

FAMILY: Malvaceae
SCIENTIFIC NAME: *Sida cordifolia*
STEMS: Erect, up to 5' tall.
LEAVES: Alternate, velvety with dense star-shaped hairs. Blades heart-shaped, up to 2¾" long.
FLOWERS: In clusters, or solitary from the leaf axils. Petals yellow to pink, up to ⅝" long.
FRUIT: Dry, splitting either partially or not at all.
HABITAT: Sandy soil, Brazos and Padre Islands.
BLOOM PERIOD: Summer, fall.

Showy Sida

FAMILY: Malvaceae
SCIENTIFIC NAME: *Sida lindheimeri*
STEMS: Erect or sprawling herbs, up to 3'
tall.
LEAVES: Alternate, the blades linear to
lanceolate, up to 2⅛" long.
FLOWERS: Solitary or clustered. Petals
yellow to pink, up to ½" or slightly
longer.
FRUIT: Dry, splitting either partially or
not at all.
HABITAT: Sandy soils, throughout the
Texas coast.
BLOOM PERIOD: Spring, summer, fall.

Woolly Globe Mallow

FAMILY: Malvaceae
SCIENTIFIC NAME: *Sphaeralcea lindheimeri*
STEMS: Sprawling, up to 30" long.
LEAVES: Alternate, velvety with soft hairs.
Blades ovate to almost heart-shaped, up to
1¾" long.
FLOWERS: Pink, the petals up to ¾" long.
FRUIT: Dry, dividing into segments that
are held together at the base.
HABITAT: Sandy soils, throughout the
Texas coast.
BLOOM PERIOD: Spring, summer.

Pyramid Flower

FAMILY: Sterculiaceae
SCIENTIFIC NAME: *Melochia pyramidata*
STEMS: Erect, usually around 12"-18" tall, but can grow up to 6½' tall.
LEAVES: Alternate, the blades ovate, toothed, up to 1¾" long.
FLOWERS: In small groups from the leaf axils. Corollas pink to violet, 5-lobed, about ¼" long.
FRUIT: A capsule, more or less pyramid-shaped, up to ¼" broad.
HABITAT: Various soils, Padre Island.
BLOOM PERIOD: Spring, summer, fall.

Hierba del Soldado

FAMILY: Sterculiaceae
SCIENTIFIC NAME: *Waltheria indica*
STEMS: Erect, hairy, 6' or taller.
LEAVES: Alternate, ovate, hairy, up to 2" long.
FLOWERS: Yellow, about ⅜" broad, in tight axillary clusters.
FRUIT: Tiny, club-shaped capsules.
HABITAT: Sandy clay, Padre Island.
BLOOM PERIOD: All seasons.

St. John's-Wort

FAMILY: Hypericaceae
SCIENTIFIC NAME: *Hypericum pauciflorum*
STEMS: More or less succulent, up to 28"
tall.
LEAVES: Opposite or whorled, linear to
lanceolate, up to 1 ¼" long and ⅛" broad.
FLOWERS: Regular, borne singly in the
leaf axils. Petals orange-yellow, about ⅜"
long.
FRUIT: Cylindrical capsules about ³⁄₁₆" tall.
HABITAT: Sandy soils, Mustang and
Matagorda Islands.
BLOOM PERIOD: Spring, summer, fall.
COMMENTS: *H. gentianoides* also grows on
some of our beaches. Its leaves are only
⅛" long, while those of *H. pauciflorum* are
longer.

Passion Flower

FAMILY: Passifloraceae
SCIENTIFIC NAME: *Passiflora foetida* var.
gossypifolia
STEMS: Hairy vines with tendrils. Stems 6'
or longer.
LEAVES: Alternate, sticky from glandular
hairs. Blades 3-lobed, up to 2¾" long.
FLOWERS: Purplish or sometimes white,
up to 2" broad.
FRUIT: Greenish-yellow and spotted,
roundish, up to 2" broad.
HABITAT: Various soils, Padre and
Matagorda Islands.
BLOOM PERIOD: Spring, summer, fall.

Texas Prickly Pear

FAMILY: Cactaceae

SCIENTIFIC NAME: *Opuntia engelmannii* var. *lindheimeri*

STEMS: Erect, up to 10' or taller, made of flattened succulent joints (pads). Many spines are present, in clusters.

LEAVES: Falling early. The spines are actually modified leaves.

FLOWERS: Bright yellow, up to 4" broad.

FRUIT: Purple when ripe, up to 2¾" long.

HABITAT: Clay-sand soils on Brazos, Padre, Mustang, and Matagorda Islands.

BLOOM PERIOD: Spring.

COMMENTS: The prickly pear flowers are very showy. Their brilliance is perhaps without equal. Inland in Cameron County, the colors vary from bright red to yellow, with all shades in between. The fruit are juicy and provide food for wild animals.

O. compressa, O. macrorhiza, and *O. stricta* also occur on the Texas beaches. They are different in that *O. compressa* usually falls over when it gets to be 3 or more joints tall; *O. macrorhiza* has spines that are mostly white or gray; and *O. stricta* is nearly spineless.

Also called *Opuntia lindheimeri.*

Tooth Cup

FAMILY: Lythraceae
SCIENTIFIC NAME: *Ammannia latifolia*
STEMS: Erect, up to 24" tall.
LEAVES: Mostly opposite, oblong or variable shape, up to 2¼" or longer.
FLOWERS: In the leaf axils, pink, less than ⅛" long.
FRUIT: Capsules ¼" or less broad.
HABITAT: Low places, Padre and Goose Islands.
BLOOM PERIOD: Spring, summer, fall.

Lanceleaf Lythrum

FAMILY: Lythraceae
SCIENTIFIC NAME: *Lythrum alatum* var. *lanceolatum*
STEMS: Erect, up to 39" tall, usually shorter.
LEAVES: Opposite, elliptic, up to 1⅜" long.
FLOWERS: Purple to reddish, with 4 to 6 petals, about ¼" long.
FRUIT: A small capsule.
HABITAT: Sandy, moist soils, Brazos, Padre, and Matagorda Islands.
BLOOM PERIOD: Spring, summer.

California Lythrum

FAMILY: Lythraceae
SCIENTIFIC NAME: *Lythrum californicum*
STEMS: Erect, up to 24" or sometimes taller.
LEAVES: Opposite, lanceolate to linear, up to ¾" long.
FLOWERS: Purple to reddish, with 4 to 6 petals, about ¼" long.
FRUIT: A small capsule.
HABITAT: Moist places, Padre and Matagorda Islands.
BLOOM PERIOD: Spring, summer.
COMMENTS: *Lythrum californicum* can be distinguished from *L. alatum* by its lighter-colored flowers and the leaves, which are usually broadest below the middle.

Square-Bud Primrose

FAMILY: Onagraceae
SCIENTIFIC NAME: *Calylophus australis*
STEMS: Erect, up to 16" tall.
LEAVES: Alternate, linear, up to 1⅛" long.
FLOWERS: Bright yellow, with 4 petals up
to ½" long.
FRUIT: A capsule about ¾" long.
HABITAT: Sandy soil, throughout the Texas
beaches.
BLOOM PERIOD: Spring, summer, fall.
COMMENTS: These plants are usually
found in large groups, producing large
masses of yellow flowers during the
blooming season.

Also known as *Calylophus serrulatus.*

Square-Bud Primrose with Indian Blanket and Mangroves

Sweet Gaura

FAMILY: Onagraceae

SCIENTIFIC NAME: *Gaura drummondii*

STEMS: Erect, up to 24" or taller.

LEAVES: Hairy, alternate, lanceolate to elliptic, up to 2¾" long. Margins variable.

FLOWERS: Bilaterally symmetrical. Sepals 4, petals 4, pink to red, up to ⅜" long.

FRUIT: Cylindrical capsules up to ¾" tall.

HABITAT: Sandy soils, Mustang Island.

BLOOM PERIOD: Spring, summer, fall.

COMMENTS: The plants are sweet-scented. Another species, *G. longiflora,* grows on Matagorda Island. In this species, the mature fruit is ¼" long or less. On *G. drummondii,* the fruit is ⅜" long or more.

Woolly Gaura

FAMILY: Onagraceae
SCIENTIFIC NAME: *Gaura villosa*
STEMS: Large, robust, and branching, up to 4' or taller.
LEAVES: Alternate, with silky hairs, more or less lanceolate, up to 2⅜" long.
FLOWERS: Petals about ½" long, white, sometimes turning pink.
FRUIT: Capsules ⅜"–¾" tall.
HABITAT: Bolivar Peninsula.
BLOOM PERIOD: Spring, summer.
COMMENTS: This species is much bigger and more robust than the other beach species of *Gaura*.

Beach Evening Primrose

FAMILY: Onagraceae

SCIENTIFIC NAME: *Oenothera drummondii*

STEMS: Erect, hairy, up to 39" tall.

LEAVES: Alternate, gray-hairy, the blades spatulate, up to 3" long.

FLOWERS: Radially symmetrical. Sepals and petals 4. Petals yellow, fading to reddish, up to 1⅜" long.

FRUIT: Capsules, cylindric, up to 1½" long.

HABITAT: Sandy clay, dunes, throughout the Texas beaches.

BLOOM PERIOD: Spring, summer, fall. The flowers open late evening.

COMMENTS: Three species of yellow evening primrose grow on the barrier islands, but they are easy to distinguish.

O. drummondii is the only one with smooth leaf margins. *O. grandis* has flowers about as big as those of *O. drummondii*, while *O. laciniata* has smaller flowers.

Showy Yellow Evening Primrose

FAMILY: Onagraceae

SCIENTIFIC NAME: *Oenothera grandis*

STEMS: Erect or leaning, up to 18" tall, usually less.

LEAVES: Alternate, the blades about 4" long, toothed and usually deeply lobed.

FLOWERS: Radially symmetrical, sepals and petals 4. Petals yellow, up to 1⅜" long.

FRUIT: A cylindric capsule up to 1⅜" long.

HABITAT: Sandy soils, Padre Island.

BLOOM PERIOD: Spring, summer.

COMMENTS: The flowers of *O. grandis* are about the same size as those of *O. drummondii,* but its toothed and lobed leaves distinguish it from that species.

Cut-Leaved Evening Primrose

FAMILY: Onagraceae
SCIENTIFIC NAME: *Oenothera laciniata*
STEMS: Erect to leaning and falling over, up to 16" tall.
LEAVES: Alternate, the blades ovate or variable, up to 3⅞" long. The margins are toothed and usually lobed.
FLOWERS: Radially symmetrical. Sepals and petals 4. The petals are yellow, up to ¾" long.
FRUIT: Cylindrical capsules up to 1⅜" long.
HABITAT: Sandy soils, Boca Chica Beach, Brazos, Padre, Mustang, and Matagorda Islands.
BLOOM PERIOD: Spring, summer.
COMMENTS: The smaller flowers of *O. laciniata* distinguish it from the other 2 yellow-flowering evening primroses.

Showy Evening Primrose

FAMILY: Onagraceae
SCIENTIFIC NAME: *Oenothera speciosa*
STEMS: Erect, often falling over, up to 12" or longer.
LEAVES: Alternate, the blades variable, obovate to lanceolate, up to 2" long. Margins toothed and lobed.
FLOWERS: Radially symmetrical. Sepals and petals 4. Petals pink, (or sometimes white), up to 1½" long.
FRUIT: Club-shaped capsules up to ⅜" long.
HABITAT: Throughout the Texas beaches.
BLOOM PERIOD: Spring, summer.
COMMENTS: This is the most common species of pink Oenotheras seen along roadsides.

Sombrerillo

FAMILY: Umbelliferae
SCIENTIFIC NAME: *Hydrocotyle bonariensis*
STEMS: Creeping, rooting at the nodes.
LEAVES: Alternate, the blades roundish, up to 2⅜" broad. Petioles are up to 12" or longer and are attached to the center of the blade rather than the edge.
FLOWERS: Very small, white to yellow, in clusters from the leaf axils, with all the pedicels arising from the same point.
FRUIT: Flattened, less than ⅛" tall.
HABITAT: Sandy soil, Boca Chica Beach, Brazos, Padre, Mustang, and Matagorda Islands.
BLOOM PERIOD: Spring, summer.
COMMENTS: Relatively few plant species have the leaf petiole attached in the center of the blade. Usually it attaches at the edge of the blade.

Scarlet Pimpernel

FAMILY: Primulaceae
SCIENTIFIC NAME: *Anagallis arvensis*
STEMS: Prostrate or sprawling.
LEAVES: Opposite, the blades ovate, up to
¾" long.
FLOWERS: Solitary, the petals blue or
sometimes salmon-colored, about ¼"
long.
FRUIT: Roundish capsules about ⅛"
broad.
HABITAT: Galveston Island. Usually in
moist soils.
BLOOM PERIOD: Late winter, spring.
COMMENTS: The common name may
seem a little strange, but in other
localities, the flowers are sometimes
scarlet.

Sea Beach Pimpernel

FAMILY: Primulaceae
SCIENTIFIC NAME: *Samolus ebracteatus*
STEMS: Erect, up to 20" tall.
LEAVES: In basal rosettes or alternate
along the stem. Blades often reddish,
spatulate, up to 3⅓" long.
FLOWERS: White or pink, about ¼" long.
FRUIT: Less than ⅛" broad, splitting open
apically.
HABITAT: Sandy soils, throughout the
Texas beaches.
BLOOM PERIOD: Spring, summer.

Sea Lavender

FAMILY: Plumbaginaceae
SCIENTIFIC NAME: *Limonium nashii*
STEMS: None.
LEAVES: In basal rosettes, spatulate, up to
8⅜" long.
FLOWERS: In highly branched
inflorescences. Petals lavender, about ¼"
long. Sepals white, remaining after petals
have fallen.

FRUIT: Very small, dry, 1-seeded.
HABITAT: Sandy clay, throughout the
Texas beaches.
BLOOM PERIOD: Summer, fall.
COMMENTS: The dried inflorescences are
often used in floral arrangements.
    Also known as *Limonium carolinianum*.

Leadwort

FAMILY: Plumbaginaceae
SCIENTIFIC NAME: *Plumbago scandens*
STEMS: Sprawling, woody, 40" or taller.
LEAVES: Alternate, the blades ovate, up to
5" long.
FLOWERS: Sepals fused, with many stalked
glands. Petals pale blue or white, basally
fused into a narrow tube ¾" long, the
upper part lobed, the flowers about ½"
broad.
FRUIT: A capsule about ⅛" or more tall.
HABITAT: Mustang Island.
BLOOM PERIOD: Spring, summer, fall.

Texas Persimmon

FAMILY: Ebenaceae

SCIENTIFIC NAME: *Diospyros texana*

STEMS: Unarmed small trees up to 19'
tall.

LEAVES: Alternate, simple. Blades obovate,
up to 2¼" long and 1" broad, hairy on
the lower surfaces.

FLOWERS: Unisexual, the male and female
flowers on separate plants. Petals white,
partially united, up to ½" long.

FRUIT: A globose, edible berry, black
when mature, about ¾" broad.

HABITAT: Sandy clay, Padre and
Matagorda Islands.

BLOOM PERIOD: Late winter, spring.

COMMENTS: The fruit are edible when
ripe. This shrub or small tree is more
often seen inland.

Polly Prim

FAMILY: Loganiaceae

SCIENTIFIC NAME: *Polypremum procumbens*

STEMS: Erect or leaning, up to 12" tall.

LEAVES: Opposite, the blades linear and up to ¾" long.

FLOWERS: Solitary, white, very tiny, about ⅛" long.

FRUIT: Globose capsules less than ⅛" broad.

HABITAT: Sandy soils, throughout the Texas beaches.

BLOOM PERIOD: Spring, summer.

Bluebell Gentian

FAMILY: Gentianaceae

SCIENTIFIC NAME: *Eustoma exaltatum*

STEMS: Erect, up to 30" tall.

LEAVES: Opposite, without petioles, the blades ovate or obovate, up to 3½" long and 1" broad.

FLOWERS: Colors from blue to white, up to ⅞" tall.

FRUIT: A cylindrical capsule about ⅝" tall.

HABITAT: Sandy clay, throughout the Texas beaches.

BLOOM PERIOD: Spring, summer.

COMMENTS: This is a very attractive wildflower. It is a relative of the Bluebell of central Texas.

Salt Marsh Pink

FAMILY: Gentianaceae
SCIENTIFIC NAME: *Sabatia arenicola*
STEMS: Erect, bushy, up to 8" tall.
LEAVES: Opposite, without petioles, elliptic to ovate, up to ⅞" long and ⅜" broad, usually broadest above the base.
FLOWERS: Pink (occasionally white) with white centers. Petals partially grown together, with lobes about ⅜" long.
FRUIT: A capsule ⅜" long.
HABITAT: Sandy soil, throughout the Texas beaches.
BLOOM PERIOD: Spring, summer.
COMMENTS: A second species (*Sabatia campestris*) grows on the barrier islands. They are very similar and often difficult to distinguish. In *S. arenicola,* the leaves are usually broadest above the base; in *S. campestris,* they are usually broadest at the base.

Meadow Pink

FAMILY: Gentianaceae
SCIENTIFIC NAME: *Sabatia campestris*
STEMS: Erect, up to 16" tall.
LEAVES: Opposite, without petioles, ovate to elliptic, up to 1¼" long and ½" broad, usually broadest at the base.
FLOWERS: Pink (occasionally white) with yellow centers. Petals partially grown together, with lobes up to ¾" long.
FRUIT: A capsule ⅜" long.
HABITAT: Sandy soil, Brazos, Padre, and Mustang Islands.
BLOOM PERIOD: Spring, summer, fall.
COMMENTS: To distinguish this species from *Sabatia arenicola,* see Comments above.

Hierba de Zizotes

FAMILY: Asclepiadaceae
SCIENTIFIC NAME: *Asclepias oenotheroides*
STEMS: Erect, about 18" tall, bleeding milky juice when broken.
LEAVES: Opposite, ovate, up to 3⅛" long, bleeding milky juice when broken.
FLOWERS: Greenish, about ¾" broad, in umbrella-like clusters from the upper leaf axils.
FRUIT: Capsules about 4" long.
HABITAT: Sandy clay, Padre, Mustang, and Matagorda Islands.
BLOOM PERIOD: Spring, summer, fall.
COMMENTS: The seeds are attached to fluffy hairs that enable them to float on a breeze.

Three other species are reported growing on our beaches. The following key can be used to identify them:

1. Leaves rounded or almost heart-shaped basally. . . . . *A. viridiflora*

1'. Leaves not as above. . . . .(2)

2. Corolla lobes not bent back. . . *A. viridis*

2'. Corolla lobes bent back . . . . (3)

3. Corolla lobes ¼" long or less . . . . *A. emoryi*

3'. Corolla lobes longer than ¼" . . . . *A. oenotheroides*

Climbing Milkweed

FAMILY: Asclepiadaceae

SCIENTIFIC NAME: *Cynanchum angustifolium*

STEMS: Perennial twining vines up to 4' or longer.

LEAVES: Alternate, somewhat succulent, the blades more or less linear, up to 3¼" long.

FLOWERS: Greenish or purplish, about ¼" broad, in umbrella-like clusters.

FRUIT: Slender, up to 2¾" long, dry and splitting open. As in *Asclepias,* the seeds are tufted with hairs that enable them to float on a breeze.

HABITAT: Moist sandy soils, Matagorda, Galveston, and Goose Islands.

BLOOM PERIOD: Spring, summer, fall.

COMMENTS: A broken part of the plant will bleed milky sap.

Leafless Cressa

FAMILY: Convolvulaceae
SCIENTIFIC NAME: *Cressa nudicaulis*
STEMS: Erect, up to 8" tall.
LEAVES: Tiny, scalelike, less than ¼" long.
FLOWERS: White, funnel-shaped, about
⅜" long.
FRUIT: A capsule with 1–4 large seeds.
HABITAT: Sandy clay, Padre and Brazos
Islands.
BLOOM PERIOD: All seasons.
COMMENTS: These plants at first glance
seem to be all stems. The leaves are
scarcely noticeable. Unlike most other
members of the family, whose flowers
have smooth margins, *Cressa* flowers are
deeply lobed.

Dodder

FAMILY: Convolvulaceae
SCIENTIFIC NAME: *Cuscuta cuspidata*
STEMS: Twining, rootless and leafless,
orange-colored.
LEAVES: None.
FLOWERS: Tiny, white.
FRUIT: A tiny, more or less globose
capsule.
HABITAT: A parasite on other plants, Padre
and Matagorda Islands.
BLOOM PERIOD: Fall.
COMMENTS: Drawing its nourishment
from other plants, *Cuscuta* does not put
roots into the ground. It does put roots
into the host plants.

Ojo de Víbora

FAMILY: Convolvulaceae
SCIENTIFIC NAME: *Evolvulus alsinoides* var.
hirticaulis
STEMS: Weak, hairy stems, mostly
prostrate.
LEAVES: Alternate, hairy, the blades
elliptic, up to ¾" long.
FLOWERS: Blue, funnel-shaped, about ⅜"
broad.
FRUIT: Small capsules, with 1–4 seeds.
HABITAT: Various sandy soils, Boca Chica
Beach, Brazos Island.
BLOOM PERIOD: All seasons.
COMMENTS: Although the flowers are
small, they are attractive and noticeable
even when mixed with other plants.

   Also called *Evolvulus alsinoides* var.
angustifolia.

Silky Evolvulus

FAMILY: Convolvulaceae
SCIENTIFIC NAME: *Evolvulus sericeus*
STEMS: Hairy and weak, usually prostrate.
LEAVES: Alternate, hairy, narrowly elliptic to linear, up to ¾" long and about ⅛" broad.
FLOWERS: White, funnel-shaped, about ⅜" broad.
FRUIT: Small capsules with 1–4 seeds.
HABITAT: Goose Island.
BLOOM PERIOD: Spring, summer, fall.
COMMENTS: The white flowers distinguish this species from *Evolvulus alsinoides* var. *hirticaulis*.

Tie Vine

FAMILY: Convolvulaceae
SCIENTIFIC NAME: *Ipomoea cordatotriloba* var. *torreyana*
STEMS: Twining vines.
LEAVES: Heart-shaped or 3–5-lobed, up to 3⅓" long and 2¾" broad.
FLOWERS: Pinkish to red-purple with darker centers, about 1¼" long, the margins smooth like the top of a funnel.

FRUIT: A capsule resembling the "woodrose" used in floral arrangements.
HABITAT: Padre and Mustang Islands.
BLOOM PERIOD: Summer, fall.
COMMENTS: This beautiful vine is often seen inland in disturbed places as well as at the coast.

Beach Morning Glory

FAMILY: Convolvulaceae

SCIENTIFIC NAME: *Ipomoea imperati*

STEMS: Prostrate, rooting at the nodes.

LEAVES: Thick and leathery. Blades about 1½" long and 2" broad, notched apically, or sometimes palmately 3–5-lobed.

FLOWERS: White with yellow centers, up to 2¾" long, the margins smooth like the top of a funnel.

FRUIT: Capsules resembling the "woodrose" used in floral arrangements.

HABITAT: Beach sands, throughout the Texas beaches.

BLOOM PERIOD: Spring, summer, fall.

COMMENTS: This widespread plant will sometimes cover the dunes with many white flowers.

In the past, it was called *Ipomoea stolonifera*.

Railroad Vine

FAMILY: Convolvulaceae
SCIENTIFIC NAME: *Ipomoea pes-caprae* var. *emarginata*
STEMS: Prostrate, rooting at the nodes, fast-growing when given plenty of moisture.
LEAVES: Thick and leathery. Blades notched apically, up to 3½" long and 4¼" broad.
FLOWERS: Purple, up to 2¾" long, the margins smooth like the top of a funnel.
FRUIT: A capsule frequently resembling the "woodrose" often used in floral arrangements.
HABITAT: Widespread, throughout the Texas beaches.

BLOOM PERIOD: Summer, fall.
COMMENTS: This plant ranks among the showiest of our coastal plants and is among the best known. One observation of stem growth over a period of a week indicated the stems grew almost 10" per day. They will grow much more slowly if moisture is lacking.

Also called *Ipomoea pes-caprae* subsp. *brasiliensis.*

Salt Marsh Morning Glory

FAMILY: Convolvulaceae
SCIENTIFIC NAME: *Ipomoea sagittata*
STEMS: Perennial twining vines up to 5½'
or longer.
LEAVES: Blades arrowhead-shaped, up to
4" long.
FLOWERS: Red-purple, up to 3½" long
and 4" or more broad, the margins
smooth like the top of a funnel.
FRUIT: A capsule frequently resembling
the "woodrose" often used in floral
arrangements.
HABITAT: Coastal marshes, Padre,
Matagorda, and Goose Islands.
BLOOM PERIOD: Spring, summer, fall.
COMMENTS: This vine is also seen inland
along creeks and riverbanks.

Alamo Vine

FAMILY: Convolvulaceae
SCIENTIFIC NAME: *Ipomoea sinuata*
STEMS: Twining vines.
LEAVES: Up to 4" long and broad, 5–7-lobed.
FLOWERS: White with purple centers, up to 2" long, the margins smooth like the top of a funnel.
FRUIT: A capsule, resembling the "woodrose" often used in floral arrangements.
HABITAT: Padre and Mustang Islands.
BLOOM PERIOD: Spring, summer, fall.
COMMENTS: This vine is often seen in disturbed places inland as well as at the coast.

Cutleaf Gilia

FAMILY: Polemoniaceae
SCIENTIFIC NAME: *Gilia incisa*
STEMS: Erect, up to 22" tall.
LEAVES: Alternate, the blades more or less
ovate, up to 2⅛" long. Margins toothed
and usually lobed.
FLOWERS: Bluish to almost white, funnel-
shaped, up to ⅜" broad.
FRUIT: A small capsule.
HABITAT: Goose Island, Matagorda Island.
BLOOM PERIOD: Spring, summer.

Rio Grande Phlox

FAMILY: Polemoniaceae

SCIENTIFIC NAME: *Phlox glabriflora* subsp. *littoralis*

STEMS: Erect or leaning, up to 12" tall.

LEAVES: Mostly linear to lanceolate, up to 2¾" long.

FLOWERS: In clusters, reddish-purple to lavender, up to 1" broad.

FRUIT: A small capsule.

HABITAT: Sand dunes, Padre and Mustang Islands.

BLOOM PERIOD: Spring, summer.

COMMENTS: *P. drummondii* also grows on Texas beaches. It has broader leaves than *P. glabriflora,* which has leaves with length 10 or more times the width.

Rough Nama

FAMILY: Hydrophyllaceae
SCIENTIFIC NAME: *Nama hispidum*
STEMS: Hairy, erect or leaning, up to 12"
tall.
LEAVES: Hairy, usually alternate, the blades
spatulate to linear, up to 2⅛" long.
FLOWERS: Single or few in a cluster, pink
to purple, funnel-shaped, ¼"–½" long.
FRUIT: A very small capsule.
HABITAT: Padre, Goose Islands.
BLOOM PERIOD: Spring.

Hairy Phacelia

FAMILY: Hydrophyllaceae
SCIENTIFIC NAME: *Phacelia hirsuta*
STEMS: Erect or leaning, hairy.
LEAVES: Alternate, hairy, oblong, up to
1¾" long and 1" broad, the margins
deeply lobed.
FLOWERS: Bluish-lavender with a whitish
center, about ½" broad.
FRUIT: A roundish capsule about ³⁄₁₆"
broad.
HABITAT: Sandy soils, Mustang Island.
BLOOM PERIOD: Spring.
COMMENTS: *P. patuliflora* is also present on
Texas beaches. Its leaves are not deeply
lobed.

Blue Phacelia

FAMILY: Hydrophyllaceae
SCIENTIFIC NAME: *Phacelia patuliflora*
STEMS: Erect to leaning, up to 12" tall.
LEAVES: Alternate, the blades ovate,
toothed, and usually lobed, up to 3" long.
FLOWERS: In 1-sided coils. Corollas
pinkish to purple with white centers, up
to 1" broad.
FRUIT: A roundish capsule about ³⁄₁₆"
broad.
HABITAT: Sandy soil, Padre Island.
BLOOM PERIOD: Spring.

Seaside Heliotrope

FAMILY: Boraginaceae

SCIENTIFIC NAME: *Heliotropium curassavicum*

STEMS: Mostly prostrate except at the tips.

LEAVES: Succulent, oblanceolate, up to 2¼" long.

FLOWERS: Small, white with yellow centers, borne on coils, the flowers on one side.

FRUIT: Small, inconspicuous, made of 4 nutlets.

HABITAT: Widespread, all the Texas beaches.

BLOOM PERIOD: All seasons.

COMMENTS: *H. convolvulaceum* (Bindweed Heliotrope) grows on Mustang Island. It is hairy and nonsucculent, and its corollas are scarcely lobed. The Seaside Heliotrope is hairless and succulent. *H. racemosum* grows on Padre Island. It is much like *H. convolvulaceum,* but its corollas are smaller and lobed.

Black Mangrove

FAMILY: Avicenniaceae

SCIENTIFIC NAME: *Avicennia germinans*

STEMS: Erect, forming shrubs up to 6' or taller.

LEAVES: Opposite, shiny, elliptic, up to 3⅛" long and 1¼" broad.

FLOWERS: Small, white, 4-lobed, in clusters.

FRUIT: Flattened, 1-seeded, greenish to gray, up to 1¼" long.

HABITAT: Wet, salty areas, widespread along the Texas coast.

BLOOM PERIOD: Summer.

COMMENTS: The black mangrove is one of the few native shrubs that grow at the coast. It is the most abundant and most noticeable of all because of the bright, shiny leaves. On mature plants, vertical branches of the roots (rhizophores) may protrude above the ground or the water.

American Beautyberry

FAMILY: Verbenaceae
SCIENTIFIC NAME: *Callicarpa americana*
STEMS: Shrubs up to 6½' tall.
LEAVES: Opposite, ovate or elliptic, up to 6" long.
FLOWERS: In axillary clusters, very small, pink.
FRUIT: Purple or violet when mature, about ¼" broad.
HABITAT: Sandy soil, Goose Island.
BLOOM PERIOD: Spring, summer.
COMMENTS: This is a beautiful, showy shrub that is often cultivated.

Dakota Vervain

FAMILY: Verbenaceae
SCIENTIFIC NAME: *Glandularia
bipinnatifida*
STEMS: Prostrate or leaning.
LEAVES: Opposite, the blades up to 1⅜"
long, divided and the first divisions
redivided.
FLOWERS: In tight clusters, the corollas
purple, up to ⅝" broad.
FRUIT: Dry, dividing into 4 nutlets.
HABITAT: Padre Island.
BLOOM PERIOD: All seasons.
COMMENTS: Formerly known as *Verbena
bipinnatifida.*

Brushland Lantana

FAMILY: Verbenaceae
SCIENTIFIC NAME: *Lantana horrida*
STEMS: Shrubs up to 6½' tall.
LEAVES: Opposite, ovate, up to 2¼" long, strong-scented when touched.
FLOWERS: In heads ¾"–1¼" broad. Individual flowers up to ⅜" broad, opening yellow, usually turning pink, orange, or red.
FRUIT: Fleshy, black or dark blue when mature, about ³⁄₁₆" broad.
HABITAT: Various soils, Brazos, Padre, Mustang, and Matagorda Islands.
BLOOM PERIOD: Spring, summer, fall.
COMMENTS: Lantana is quite variable in its color. Some plants will have flowers that remain yellow. Others will have flowers turning to pink, to orange, or to red. Since the flowers in a head open consecutively and gradually change color after opening, the effect is of a small bouquet of flowers ranging from yellow to the final color.

Also known as *Lantana urticoides*.

Texas Frog Fruit

FAMILY: Verbenaceae

SCIENTIFIC NAME: *Phyla nodiflora*

STEMS: Prostrate perennials, sometimes woody basally, up to 24" or longer.

LEAVES: Opposite, lanceolate, up to 1½" long.

FLOWERS: In cylindrical heads arising from the leaf axils. Individual flowers white with yellow or purple centers, about ⅛" broad.

FRUIT: Very small, dry, separating into 2 nutlets.

HABITAT: Sandy clay, Padre, Mustang, and Matagorda Islands.

BLOOM PERIOD: Spring, summer, fall.

COMMENTS: The two *Phyla* species are very similar. They are easily distinguished by leaf characteristics. *P. nodiflora* has a leaf length (with petiole) 5 or more times the width. *P. strigulosa* has a leaf length (with petiole) 4 or fewer times the width. A third species, *P. lanceolata,* grows on Padre Island. The teeth on its leaves extend down below the middle; those of the other two species do not.

Frog Fruit

FAMILY: Verbenaceae

SCIENTIFIC NAME: *Phyla strigulosa*

STEMS: Prostrate perennials, sometimes woody basally, up to 22" or longer.

LEAVES: Opposite, obovate to ovate, up to 1¾" long.

FLOWERS: In cylindrical heads arising from the leaf axils. Individual flowers white with yellow or purple centers, about ⅛" broad.

FRUIT: Very small, dry, separating into 2 nutlets.

HABITAT: Sandy soil, Padre Island.

BLOOM PERIOD: Spring, summer, fall.

Brazilian Vervain

FAMILY: Verbenaceae
SCIENTIFIC NAME: *Verbena brasiliensis*
STEMS: Erect, 4'–8' tall.
LEAVES: Opposite, usually toothed and lobed, about 4" long.
FLOWERS: In compact spikes, the corollas about ⅛" broad.
FRUIT: Small, dry, dividing into 4 nutlets.
HABITAT: Sandy clay, Bolivar Peninsula.
BLOOM PERIOD: Spring, summer, fall.
COMMENTS: This species grows much taller than *V. officinalis,* and its flowers are smaller.

Texas Vervain

FAMILY: Verbenaceae
SCIENTIFIC NAME: *Verbena officinalis*
STEMS: Erect. Up to 39" tall.
LEAVES: Opposite, usually toothed and lobed.
FLOWERS: Small, loosely arranged on erect bloom stalks. Corollas blue, about ⁵⁄₁₆" broad.
FRUIT: Small, dry, dividing into 4 nutlets.
HABITAT: Boca Chica Beach; Brazos, Padre, Mustang, Matagorda, and Galveston Islands.
BLOOM PERIOD: Spring, summer, fall.
COMMENTS: Also known as *Verbena halei.*

Lemon Beebalm

FAMILY: Labiatae
SCIENTIFIC NAME: *Monarda citriodora*
STEMS: Erect, up to 32" tall.
LEAVES: Narrowly elliptic to lanceolate, up to 2⅛" long and ½" or more broad.
FLOWERS: White to pink, about ¾" long, in dense axillary clusters. Petals partially grown together.
FRUIT: Divided into 4 segments called nutlets.
HABITAT: Various soils, Padre and Mustang Islands.
BLOOM PERIOD: Spring, summer, fall.
COMMENTS: The plants have a citrus or lemon odor.

Skullcap

FAMILY: Labiatae
SCIENTIFIC NAME: *Scutellaria muriculata*
STEMS: Erect, up to 12" tall.
LEAVES: Opposite, simple, the blades ovate, up to ⅝" long.
FLOWERS: Single or few from the leaf axils. Petals partially grown together to form a 2-lipped, blue to violet flower up to ⅝" long.
FRUIT: Divided into 4 dry segments called nutlets.
HABITAT: Sandy areas, Padre and Matagorda Islands.
BLOOM PERIOD: Spring, summer, fall.
COMMENTS: The genus is recognized by a lip or ridge on the upper calyx.

Small Coast Germander

FAMILY: Labiatae

SCIENTIFIC NAME: *Teucrium cubense*

STEMS: Erect, up to 28" tall.

LEAVES: Opposite, simple, the blades ovate, up to 1¾" long and ¾" broad, with toothed and lobed margins.

FLOWERS: In apical spikes. Petals partially grown together to form a 2-lipped, white flower up to ⅝" long.

FRUIT: Divided into 4 dry segments called nutlets.

HABITAT: Sandy clay, Padre and Matagorda Islands.

BLOOM PERIOD: All seasons.

Carolina Wolfberry

FAMILY: Solanaceae
SCIENTIFIC NAME: *Lycium carolinianum*
var. *quadrifidum*
STEMS: Shrubs up to 40" tall or less.
LEAVES: Alternate, the blades spatulate, up
to 1½" long.
FLOWERS: Single or few from the leaf
axils. Corollas bluish, usually 4-lobed, up
to ⅜" long.
FRUIT: A berry, about ⅜" broad, red when
mature.
HABITAT: Sandy soils, Boca Chica Beach;
Brazos, Padre, Mustang, and Matagorda
Islands; Bolivar Peninsula.
BLOOM PERIOD: Spring, summer, fall.
COMMENTS: Most of our plants in the
Solanaceae family have 5-lobed corollas.
Carolina Wolfberry is distinctive in having
the 4-lobed corollas.

Netted Globe Berry

FAMILY: Solanaceae

SCIENTIFIC NAME: *Margaranthus solanaceus*

STEMS: Erect, up to 24" tall.

LEAVES: Alternate, the blades more or less ovate, up to 2⅜" long.

FLOWERS: Usually single from the leaf axils. Corollas greenish yellow or purplish, about ⅛" long.

FRUIT: A berry about ³⁄₁₆" broad, red when mature. It is enclosed in a papery balloon formed by the calyx.

HABITAT: Sandy clay, Padre Island.

BLOOM PERIOD: Spring, summer, fall.

COMMENTS: This species and the Ground Cherry (*Physalis viscosa*) both have the papery calyx forming a balloon around the fruit. The Ground Cherry has much bigger flowers.

Tree Tobacco

FAMILY: Solanaceae
SCIENTIFIC NAME: *Nicotiana glauca*
STEMS: Shrubs or small trees sometimes almost 10' tall.
LEAVES: Alternate, the blades leathery, ovate, up to 3¾" long.
FLOWERS: Greenish-yellow, tube-shaped, up to 1½" long.
FRUIT: Egg-shaped, ½" tall or less.
HABITAT: Sandy soil, Padre Island.
BLOOM PERIOD: Spring, summer, fall.

Wild Tobacco

FAMILY: Solanaceae
SCIENTIFIC NAME: *Nicotiana repanda*
STEMS: Erect, up to 40" tall, usually less. Stems and leaves are sticky with glandular hairs.
LEAVES: Basal leaves are ovate to spatulate, up to 12½" long.
FLOWERS: Flower clusters emerge from the apex. Corollas white, with long tubes, up to 3⅛" long.
FRUIT: A capsule about ⅜" long.
HABITAT: Sandy clay, Padre Island.
BLOOM PERIOD: Spring, summer, fall.
COMMENTS: *N. glauca* grows on Padre Island. It is a shrub with yellow tube flowers.

Ground Cherry

FAMILY: Solanaceae
SCIENTIFIC NAME: *Physalis cinerascens* var. *cinerascens*
STEMS: Erect to leaning or sprawling, up to 12" or longer, with star-shaped hairs.
LEAVES: Alternate, ovate, up to 2¾" long, with star-shaped hairs.
FLOWERS: Single from the leaf axils. Corollas yellowish with dark purple centers, 5-lobed, about ¾" broad.
FRUIT: A berry about ¾" broad, red when mature. It is enclosed in a papery balloon formed by the calyx.
HABITAT: Sandy soil, Galveston Island.
BLOOM PERIOD: All seasons.
COMMENTS: The two varieties are easily distinguished by their leaf shapes. The var. *spathulaefolia* is more widespread on the sandy coast, while the var. *cinerascens* is more common inland.

Ground Cherry

FAMILY: Solanaceae

SCIENTIFIC NAME: *Physalis cinerascens* var. *spathulaefolia*

STEMS: Erect to leaning, hairy, up to 12" tall.

LEAVES: Alternate, more or less spatulate, up to 3½" long.

FLOWERS: Single from the leaf axils. Corollas yellowish with dark purple centers, 5-lobed, about ¾" broad.

FRUIT: A berry about ¾" broad, red when mature. It is enclosed in a papery balloon formed by the calyx.

HABITAT: Beach sand, throughout the Texas beaches.

BLOOM PERIOD: All seasons.

COMMENTS: This species is easily distinguished from Netted Globe Berry (*Margaranthus solanaceus*) by its much bigger flowers.

American Nightshade

FAMILY: Solanaceae
SCIENTIFIC NAME: *Solanum americanum*
STEMS: Weak and often sprawling, up to 20" long.
LEAVES: Alternate, the blades triangular to ovate, up to 4" long.
FLOWERS: In small groups. Corollas white, often tinged with purple, 5-lobed, up to $\frac{5}{16}$" broad.
FRUIT: A berry up to $\frac{5}{16}$" broad, black when mature.
HABITAT: Various soils, Padre and Matagorda Islands.
BLOOM PERIOD: All seasons.

Silverleaf Nightshade

FAMILY: Solanaceae
SCIENTIFIC NAME: *Solanum elaeagnifolium*
STEMS: Erect, often prickly, up to 24" tall.
LEAVES: Alternate, the blades ovate, up to 4⅛" long.
FLOWERS: In groups up to 5. Corollas purple to bluish or white, 5-lobed, up to 1" broad.
FRUIT: A berry up to ⅝" broad, brownish or black when mature.
HABITAT: Various soils, throughout the Texas coast.
BLOOM PERIOD: Spring, summer, fall.
COMMENTS: This species is very widespread in Texas.

Texas Nightshade

FAMILY: Solanaceae
SCIENTIFIC NAME: *Solanum triquetrum*
STEMS: Spindly, clambering, up to 66" long, 3-cornered when young.
LEAVES: Alternate, the blades triangular, up to 1⅛" long, sometimes with basal lobes.
FLOWERS: In small groups. Corollas white, sometimes tinged with purple, 5-lobed, up to ⅝" broad.
FRUIT: A berry up to ⅝" broad, red when mature.
HABITAT: Various soils, Padre and Matagorda Islands.
BLOOM PERIOD: Spring, summer, fall.

Prairie Agalinis

FAMILY: Scrophulariaceae
SCIENTIFIC NAME: *Agalinis heterophylla*
STEMS: Erect, up to 39" tall.
LEAVES: Opposite below, sometimes alternate higher on the stem. Blades linear, up to 1½" long.
FLOWERS: In the leaf axils or terminal clusters. Corollas partially grown together to form a 5-lobed, pink to white, bilateral corolla up to 1½" long.
FRUIT: A capsule about ¼" tall.
HABITAT: Sand or sandy clay, Brazos and Padre Islands.
BLOOM PERIOD: Spring, summer.
COMMENTS: Four species of *Agalinis* are found on the beaches and islands. *A. fasciculata* is the only one with rough stems. *A. heterophylla* has calyx lobes about half the total length of the calyx. Of the remaining two, *A. maritima* has succulent, crowded leaves, while the leaves on *A. strictifolia* are neither succulent nor crowded.

An older name for the genus is *Gerardia*.

Growing between the dune systems

Water–Hyssop

FAMILY: Scrophulariaceae

SCIENTIFIC NAME: *Bacopa monnieri*

STEMS: Creeping or floating, about 6" long.

LEAVES: Opposite, spatulate, succulent, up to ⅝" long.

FLOWERS: In the leaf axils, white to pale blue, up to ⅜" long.

FRUIT: A capsule less than ¼" long.

HABITAT: Moist places throughout the Texas beaches.

BLOOM PERIOD: Spring, summer, fall.

Texas Paintbrush

FAMILY: Scrophulariaceae
SCIENTIFIC NAME: *Castilleja indivisa*
STEMS: Erect, hairy, up to 16" tall.
LEAVES: Alternate, lanceolate to linear, up to 4" long.
FLOWERS: Corollas bilateral, mostly greenish, with the petals partially grown together. Flowers enclosed in showy bracts colored bright orange-red.
FRUIT: A small, many-seeded capsule.
HABITAT: Sandy soil, Padre and Mustang Islands.
BLOOM PERIOD: Spring.

Cenizo

FAMILY: Scrophulariaceae

SCIENTIFIC NAME: *Leucophyllum frutescens*

STEMS: Shrubs 6' tall or more.

LEAVES: Alternate, silvery with dense white hairs. Blades ovate, up to ¾" long.

FLOWERS: Pinkish to purplish color, rarely white, about 1¼" long, lobed. Petals grown together in the lower part of the flower, forming a tube.

FRUIT: A small capsule.

HABITAT: Goose Island.

BLOOM PERIOD: Spring, summer, fall. Usually blooms after rains.

COMMENTS: This is a very attractive shrub, and it is often cultivated for its beauty and easy care.

Texas Toadflax

FAMILY: Scrophulariaceae
SCIENTIFIC NAME: *Linaria texana*
STEMS: Erect, up to 22" tall.
LEAVES: Opposite basally, alternate higher on the stem. Blades linear, up to 1⅜" long.
FLOWERS: In terminal groups. Petals partially united to form a 5-lobed, violet-colored corolla about ½" long with a slender basal spur.
FRUIT: A capsule about ⅛" tall.
HABITAT: Sandy soils, Padre, Mustang, and Matagorda Islands.
BLOOM PERIOD: Spring, summer, fall.
COMMENTS: Also known as *Nuttallanthus texanus*.

Vine Snapdragon

FAMILY: Scrophulariaceae
SCIENTIFIC NAME: *Maurandya antirrhiniflora*
STEMS: Twining vines, 40" or longer.
LEAVES: Alternate to nearly opposite. Blades arrowhead-shaped, up to 1" long.
FLOWERS: In the leaf axils, the petals purple to whitish, partially grown together to form a 5-lobed corolla.
FRUIT: A capsule about 3⁄16" long.
HABITAT: Various soils, Padre, Mustang, and Matagorda Islands.
BLOOM PERIOD: Spring, summer.

Photographed at Lady Bird Johnson Wildflower Center, Austin, Texas

Yellow Mecardonia

FAMILY: Scrophulariaceae
SCIENTIFIC NAME: *Mecardonia vandellioides*
STEMS: Erect or leaning, up to 6" tall.
LEAVES: Opposite, the blades variable, up to ⅞" long.
FLOWERS: In the leaf axils, petals yellow, partially grown together to form a 5-lobed corolla.
FRUIT: A small capsule.
HABITAT: Goose Island.
BLOOM PERIOD: All seasons.
COMMENTS: Also known as *Mecardonia procumbens*.

Woolly Stemodia

FAMILY: Scrophulariaceae
SCIENTIFIC NAME: *Stemodia lanata*
STEMS: Prostrate, forming mats 40" or more across.
LEAVES: Opposite, white or silvery with dense hairs. Blades obovate, up to ¾" long.
FLOWERS: Mostly solitary, purplish, up to ¼" or slightly longer, the petals grown together to form a 5-lobed corolla.
FRUIT: A very small capsule.
HABITAT: Sandy soils, Boca Chica Beach, Brazos, Padre, Mustang, and Matagorda Islands.
BLOOM PERIOD: Spring, summer.

Broomrape

FAMILY: Orobanchaceae
SCIENTIFIC NAME: *Orobanche ludoviciana* var. *multiflora*
STEMS: Erect, 8" or taller.
LEAVES: Alternate, whitish, scalelike, about ⅜" long.
FLOWERS: Bilaterally symmetrical, up to 1⅜" long. Petals purple to yellow.
FRUIT: A capsule about ⅝" long.
HABITAT: Sandy soil, Boca Chica Beach, Padre and Brazos Islands.
BLOOM PERIOD: Spring, summer.
COMMENTS: This plant is a root parasite.
Also known as *Orobanche multiflora*.

Red-Seeded Plantain

FAMILY: Plantaginaceae
SCIENTIFIC NAME: *Plantago rhodosperma*
STEMS: None.
LEAVES: In a basal rosette. Blades
oblanceolate, up to 12¾" long.
FLOWERS: Tiny, in cylindrical clusters,
mostly hidden by scaly bracts.
FRUIT: A spherical capsule, splitting
around the middle. The seeds are red.
HABITAT: Various soils, throughout the
Texas coast.
BLOOM PERIOD: Spring.
COMMENTS: Other species grow on the
Texas coast. Their identification usually
requires use of technical characteristics.

Buttonbush

FAMILY: Rubiaceae
SCIENTIFIC NAME: *Cephalanthus occidentalis* var. *californicus*
STEMS: Shrubs or small trees up to 10' or taller, usually less.
LEAVES: Opposite, the blades ovate, up to 5¼" long and 2" broad.
FLOWERS: In dense spherical heads about 1¼" broad. Corollas white.
FRUIT: Small, with 1 seed.
HABITAT: Marshes, moist places, Padre and Goose Islands.
BLOOM PERIOD: Summer.

Rough Buttonweed

FAMILY: Rubiaceae
SCIENTIFIC NAME: *Diodia teres*
STEMS: Erect or leaning, up to 30" tall.
LEAVES: Opposite, the blades lanceolate, up to 1⅜" long.
FLOWERS: Usually single, occasionally few in the leaf axils. Corollas white to purplish, about ¼" broad.
FRUIT: Small, leathery, splitting open.
HABITAT: Sandy soils, Padre and Matagorda Islands.
BLOOM PERIOD: Spring, summer, fall.
COMMENTS: This species has noticeably smaller flowers than *D. virginiana*.

Virginia Buttonweed

FAMILY: Rubiaceae
SCIENTIFIC NAME: *Diodia virginiana*
STEMS: Leaning or prostrate, with branches up to 24" long.
LEAVES: Opposite, more or less elliptical, up to 2¾" long.
FLOWERS: White, from the leaf axils, about ⅜" broad.
FRUIT: Almost ⅜" tall, with 2 or 3 small points (the persistent calyx teeth) at the top.
HABITAT: Matagorda and Galveston Islands, Bolivar Peninsula.
BLOOM PERIOD: Spring, summer, fall.

Clingon Bedstraw

FAMILY: Rubiaceae
SCIENTIFIC NAME: *Galium aparine*
STEMS: Sprawling, with stiff downward-curved bristles.
LEAVES: In whorls of 6–8, the blades spatulate, up to 1⅛" long.
FLOWERS: Single, or up to 3 together. Corollas white, less than ⅛" broad.
FRUIT: Bristly, about ⅛" broad.
HABITAT: Galveston Island.
BLOOM PERIOD: Spring.

Bluet

FAMILY: Rubiaceae
SCIENTIFIC NAME: *Hedyotis nigricans*
STEMS: Erect to leaning or falling over.
LEAVES: Opposite, up to ¾" long and very narrow, ⅛" broad or less.
FLOWERS: 5 to 15 per inflorescence. Petals 4, white or bluish, less than ⅜" long.
FRUIT: Very small, dry.
HABITAT: Loose sand to sandy clay, Brazos, Padre, and Matagorda Islands.
BLOOM PERIOD: Spring, summer.
COMMENTS: Two other species that grow on the barrier islands may be confused with *Hedyotis nigricans*. All three species have the same general appearance. The flowers are small, white or bluish, with 4 sepals and 4 petals. The leaves are small and narrow.

H. subviscosa has solitary flowers, whereas *H. nigricans* has several flowers per inflorescence.

Polypremum procumbens has a superior ovary (the petals and sepals are attached below the ovary), whereas both *Hedyotis* species have an inferior ovary (the petals and sepals are grown to the ovary, seeming to originate from the top of the ovary).

White Girdlepod

FAMILY: Rubiaceae
SCIENTIFIC NAME: *Mitracarpus breviflorus*
STEMS: More or less erect, up to 16" tall.
LEAVES: Opposite. Blades lanceolate, up to
1⅛" long.
FLOWERS: Clustered in the leaf axils.
Corollas white, 4-lobed, about ¼" long.
FRUIT: Capsules tiny, splitting around the
middle.
HABITAT: Sandy soil, Brazos and Padre
Islands.
BLOOM PERIOD: Summer, fall.
COMMENTS: *Mitracarpus* is similar to
Diodia and *Richardia*. Its capsules split
around the middle, whereas the capsules
of *Diodia* and *Richardia* split from top to
bottom.

Richardia

FAMILY: Rubiaceae
SCIENTIFIC NAME: *Richardia brasiliensis*
STEMS: Prostrate or leaning, up to 28"
long.
LEAVES: Opposite. Blades ovate, up to 1½"
long.
FLOWERS: In terminal clusters. Corollas
white, about ⅜" broad, 5–7-lobed.
FRUIT: Capsules very small, splitting from
top to bottom.
HABITAT: Sandy soil throughout the Texas
beaches.
BLOOM PERIOD: Spring, summer, fall.

Japanese Honeysuckle

FAMILY: Caprifoliaceae
SCIENTIFIC NAME: *Lonicera japonica*
STEMS: Climbing vines, the stems becoming woody.
LEAVES: Opposite, ovate, up to 3⅛" long.
FLOWERS: White, turning yellow, up to 1⅛" long. Fragrant.
FRUIT: Black berries about ¼" broad.
HABITAT: Growing on fences, shrubs, trees, Galveston Island.
BLOOM PERIOD: Spring, summer.
COMMENTS: Native of Asia, escaped from cultivation.

Elderberry

FAMILY: Caprifoliaceae
SCIENTIFIC NAME: *Sambucus canadensis*
STEMS: Erect, somewhat woody, up to 6½' tall.
LEAVES: Opposite, compound, the leaflets about 4" long.
FLOWERS: White, in flattened clusters.
FRUIT: Purplish black, about ⅛" or slightly broader.
HABITAT: Usually in moist places, Galveston Island.
BLOOM PERIOD: Spring, early summer.
COMMENTS: The fruit is edible and is used to make jelly.

Globe Berry

FAMILY: Cucurbitaceae
SCIENTIFIC NAME: *Ibervillea lindheimeri*
STEMS: Vines with tendrils.
LEAVES: Blades up to 3⅛" long and broad, mostly deeply 3-lobed.
FLOWERS: Yellowish, the male flowers in clusters and the female flowers solitary, on separate plants.
FRUIT: A spherical orange to red berry, up to 1⅜" broad.
HABITAT: Padre and Matagorda Islands.
BLOOM PERIOD: Spring, summer.
COMMENTS: These plants are in the gourd family, and their leaves and fruit resemble those of squash or a gourd.

Melonette

FAMILY: Cucurbitaceae
SCIENTIFIC NAME: *Melothria pendula*
STEMS: Hairy, climbing or trailing vines with tendrils.
LEAVES: Alternate, heart-shaped, up to 2¾" long and broad.
FLOWERS: Male and female flowers on the same plant. Corollas yellow, about ⅛" broad.
FRUIT: Cylindrical, up to ¾" long, resembling a tiny watermelon.
HABITAT: Padre, Matagorda, and Galveston Islands. Various soils.
BLOOM PERIOD: Spring, summer, fall.

Western Ragweed

FAMILY: Compositae
SCIENTIFIC NAME: *Ambrosia psilostachya*
STEMS: Erect, 24" or taller.
LEAVES: Opposite below, alternate above.
Petioles indistinct. Blades up to 3½" or
longer, deeply lobed.
FLOWERS: Male and female flowers tiny,
on separate heads, but on the same plant.
Flower heads about ⅛" broad, in clusters
and hanging downward.
FRUIT: An achene, small and dry, without
pappus.
HABITAT: Sandy areas throughout the
Texas coast.
BLOOM PERIOD: Summer, fall.
COMMENTS: The Compositae family
(Sunflower family), also known as the
Asteraceae, has some unusual
characteristics. If the reader is not already
familiar with this family, detailed
information can be found in the
Introduction.

Ambrosia psilostachya does not follow the
typical pattern of the Sunflower family.
The flowers are very small, hidden within
enclosing bracts (the involucre). They are
not showy. The pollen from this and other
ragweeds is extremely allergenic, causing
much suffering to those who are sensitive
to it.

Broomweed

FAMILY: Compositae
SCIENTIFIC NAME: *Amphiachyris dracunculoides*
STEMS: Erect, up to 40" tall, but usually shorter.
LEAVES: Alternate, resinous, linear, up to ¾" or longer.
FLOWERS: In heads about ½" broad. Ray flowers yellow, ⅛" long; disk flowers yellow.
FRUIT: A tiny achene, flattened, usually hairy, the pappus tiny and inconspicuous.
HABITAT: In sandy clay throughout the Texas coast.
BLOOM PERIOD: Fall.
COMMENTS: Formerly known as *Xanthocephalum dracunculoides.*

Photographed on Galveston Island

Lazy Daisy

FAMILY: Compositae
SCIENTIFIC NAME: *Aphanostephus skirrhobasis*
STEMS: Up to 18" tall, but weak and falling over.
LEAVES: Alternate, usually lobed or toothed, the blades up to 2¾" long and ⅝" broad.
FLOWERS: In heads up to 1" broad. Ray flowers white, ⅜" long; disk flowers yellow.
FRUIT: A tiny achene about ¹⁄₁₆" tall, the pappus inconspicuous or absent.
HABITAT: Sandy soils, throughout the Texas beaches.
BLOOM PERIOD: Spring, summer.
COMMENTS: There are three named varieties that are difficult to distinguish. The most widespread is var. *thalassius.*

Aster

FAMILY: Compositae

SCIENTIFIC NAME: *Aster subulatus* var. *ligulatus*

STEMS: Erect, up to 39" tall.

LEAVES: Up to 6" long and ½" broad, usually smaller.

FLOWERS: In heads up to ¾" broad. Ray flowers white or bluish, ⅜" long. Disk flowers yellow.

FRUIT: A somewhat flattened achene ⅜" long with pappus bristles ⅛" long.

HABITAT: Sands of Padre Island, Brazos Island, and Boca Chica Beach.

BLOOM PERIOD: Summer, fall.

COMMENTS: These plants may be very tall and bushy, or, if they have been cut or broken, may bloom when only a few inches tall.

Also known as *Symphyotrichum divaricatum*.

Roosevelt Weed

FAMILY: Compositae
SCIENTIFIC NAME: *Baccharis salicina*
STEMS: Shrubs sometimes almost 10' tall.
LEAVES: Alternate, the blades linear or
narrowly elliptic, up to 3⅛" long.
FLOWERS: Very small but numerous,
whitish, male and female flowers on
separate plants.
FRUIT: Achenes less than ⅛" tall, with
pappus bristles up to ⅜" long.
HABITAT: Various, often quite "weedy."
Padre Island.
BLOOM PERIOD: Fall.
COMMENTS: Also known as *Baccharis
salicifolia*.

Sea Ox Eye

FAMILY: Compositae
SCIENTIFIC NAME: *Borrichia frutescens*
STEMS: Erect, woody, up to 32" tall.
LEAVES: Opposite, without petioles, up to
2¼" long and ¾" broad.
FLOWERS: In heads up to 1⅛" broad. Ray
flowers yellow, up to ⅜" long. Disk
flowers yellow.
FRUIT: Achenes 3- or 4-sided, ⅛" tall,
with pappus of 2 very short scales.
HABITAT: Widespread and abundant along
the Texas coast, in sandy clay.
BLOOM PERIOD: All seasons.
COMMENTS: These plants are usually
found in large stands rather than scattered
individual plants. They are very attractive.

Straggler Daisy

FAMILY: Compositae
SCIENTIFIC NAME: *Calyptocarpus vialis*
STEMS: Weak, creeping along the ground.
LEAVES: Opposite, the blades ovate, up to
1¾" long, usually less.
FLOWERS: In heads ¼" broad or slightly
bigger. Ray flowers yellow, disk flowers
yellow.
FRUIT: Achenes flattened, tapering, ⅛" tall
or less, with 2 tiny awns at the top.
HABITAT: Roadsides, in gardens, Goose
Island, Galveston Island.
BLOOM PERIOD: All seasons.
COMMENTS: This small but attractive plant
is very invasive, often turning up in
gardens and along walkways.

Basket Flower

FAMILY: Compositae
SCIENTIFIC NAME: *Centaurea americana*
STEMS: Erect, up to 5' tall.
LEAVES: Alternate, without petioles.
Blades lanceolate, up to 8" long.
FLOWERS: In heads 2½"–4" broad. Ray
flowers absent. Disk flowers pinkish, rarely
white.
FRUIT: Achenes flattened, about ⅛" tall.
Pappus bristles about ¼" long.
HABITAT: Sandy soils, Padre Island.
BLOOM PERIOD: Spring, summer.
COMMENTS: The bracts enclosing the
flower heads have a basketlike appearance,
giving the plant its common name.

Bull Thistle

FAMILY: Compositae
SCIENTIFIC NAME: *Cirsium horridulum* var.
elliottii
STEMS: Erect, up to 40" tall.
LEAVES: Very spiny, up to 12" long.
FLOWERS: In heads 3" broad or larger.
Ray flowers absent. Disk flowers pink
shades, to purple or white, occasionally
yellow.
FRUIT: Achenes flattened, about ¼" long.
Pappus bristles about ¾" long.
HABITAT: Growing in sand, Padre,
Mustang, Goose, Matagorda, and
Galveston Islands.
BLOOM PERIOD: Spring, summer.
COMMENTS: *C. horridulum* has larger
heads of flowers than *C. texanum,* and its
heads are subtended by a whorl of spiny
bracts.

Thistle

FAMILY: Compositae
SCIENTIFIC NAME: *Cirsium texanum*
STEMS: Erect, up to 5½' tall.
LEAVES: Up to 18" long and 6" broad, lobed, each lobe tipped with a stiff, sharp spine.
FLOWERS: In heads up to 2¾" broad. Ray flowers absent. Disk flowers pink.
FRUIT: Achenes about ¼" tall. Pappus bristles about ¾" long.
HABITAT: Sandy clay, Padre Island.
BLOOM PERIOD: Spring, summer.
COMMENTS: *C. texanum* and *C. horridulum* are similar in appearance, but are easily distinguished. They are compared in the description of the latter species.

Clappia

FAMILY: Compositae
SCIENTIFIC NAME: *Clappia suaedifolia*
STEMS: Erect, up to 18" tall.
LEAVES: Alternate except at the base of
the stem. Blades linear, up to 2¼" long
and ⅛" broad.
FLOWERS: In solitary heads 1"–1½"
broad. Ray flowers yellow, about ⅜" long.
Disk flowers yellow.
FRUIT: Achenes about ⅛" tall, with
pappus bristles ³⁄₁₆" long.
HABITAT: Salty areas, Padre Island.
BLOOM PERIOD: Spring, fall.
COMMENTS: This species is more
abundant south into Mexico.

Horse Weed

FAMILY: Compositae
SCIENTIFIC NAME: *Conyza canadensis*
STEMS: Erect, up to 39" or taller.
LEAVES: Alternate, linear, without petioles,
1¾" long or sometimes longer, about ⅛"
broad.
FLOWERS: In numerous small heads about
³⁄₁₆" tall.
FRUIT: Achenes less than ¹⁄₁₆" tall, with
pappus bristles about ¹⁄₁₆" long.
HABITAT: Disturbed places, Padre Island.
BLOOM PERIOD: Spring, summer, fall.
COMMENTS: *Conyza canadensis* is either
hairless or with hairs that point straight
out. *C. ramosissima,* another beach species,
has hairs that are flattened against the
stem.

Conyza

FAMILY: Compositae

SCIENTIFIC NAME: *Conyza ramosissima*

STEMS: Erect, much branched, usually 3'–4' tall.

LEAVES: More or less linear, up to ½" long and ⅛" broad.

FLOWERS: In numerous small heads borne toward the top of the plant. The heads are cream-colored and ⅛" tall or slightly more. The ray flowers and disk flowers are very similar.

FRUIT: Achenes about ¹⁄₁₆" tall with pappus bristles about the same length.

HABITAT: Sandy clay, Padre Island, Bolivar Peninsula.

BLOOM PERIOD: Summer and fall.

COMMENTS: It is a little unusual to find this species growing on the coast. According to B. L. Turner, of the University of Texas at Austin, it is generally found farther inland in Texas.

Coreopsis

FAMILY: Compositae
SCIENTIFIC NAME: *Coreopsis basalis*
STEMS: Erect, about 16" tall, hairy basally.
LEAVES: Opposite, the larger ones compound, up to 6" long, with the leaflets linear to ovate.
FLOWERS: In heads up to 2⅛" broad. Ray flowers yellow with brownish red basal spots. Disk flowers dark reddish purple apically.
FRUIT: Achenes about ⅛" long with pappus of 2 small pointed scales.
HABITAT: Sandy areas, Goose Island, Galveston Island.
BLOOM PERIOD: Spring, summer.
COMMENTS: *Coreopsis tinctoria* also grows on the Texas coast. Its stems are not hairy. *C. basalis* usually has hairy stems toward the base. *C. nuecensis,* a third beach species, has yellow disk flowers. The other two species have brown or purplish disk flowers.

Tickseed

FAMILY: Compositae
SCIENTIFIC NAME: *Coreopsis nuecensis*
STEMS: Erect, up to 16" tall, sparsely hairy, or almost hairless.
LEAVES: Basal, or opposite on the lower part of the stem. Blades compound or simple, up to 4¾" long.
FLOWERS: In heads up to 2" broad. Ray flowers yellow, turning orange toward the base. A ring of variable reddish dots or lines separates the yellow from the orange color. Disk flowers yellow, sometimes light brown.
FRUIT: Achenes abut ⅛" tall, with a pappus of 2 small pointed scales.
HABITAT: Sandy soils, Padre Island.
BLOOM PERIOD: Spring.

Golden Wave

FAMILY: Compositae
SCIENTIFIC NAME: *Coreopsis tinctoria*
STEMS: Erect, 20" tall or more.
LEAVES: Opposite, compound, the blades
4" long, the leaflets mostly linear.
FLOWERS: In heads about 1⅛" broad. Ray
flowers yellow, usually with a red spot
basally. Disk flowers reddish brown.
FRUIT: Achenes about ⅛" tall, with a
pappus of 2 small pointed scales.
HABITAT: Sandy soil, Padre and
Matagorda Islands.
BLOOM PERIOD: Spring, summer, fall.
COMMENTS: See comments above to
distinguish *C. tinctoria* from *C. basalis.*

Corpus Christi Fleabane

FAMILY: Compositae
SCIENTIFIC NAME: *Erigeron procumbens*
STEMS: Prostrate, rooting at the nodes.
LEAVES: Alternate, the blades spatulate, up
to 3⅛" long and 1" broad. Margins lobed
or toothed.
FLOWERS: In heads about ¾" broad. Ray
flowers white or bluish, about ⁵⁄₁₆" long.
Disk flowers yellow.
FRUIT: Achenes less than ¹⁄₁₆" long with
bristles up to ⅛" long.
HABITAT: Sandy soils throughout the
Texas beaches.
BLOOM PERIOD: Spring, summer.
COMMENTS: Formerly known as *Erigeron
myrionactis.*

Azure Boneset

FAMILY: Compositae
SCIENTIFIC NAME: *Eupatorium azureum*
STEMS: Woody, sprawling, up to 10' long.
LEAVES: Opposite, the blades triangular or
ovate, up to 2⅜" long.
FLOWERS: In heads about ⅜" tall. There
are no ray flowers. Disk flowers are bluish,
rarely white.
FRUIT: Achenes tiny, less than ⅛" tall, with
bristles about ⅛" long.
HABITAT: Disturbed areas, Galveston
Island.
BLOOM PERIOD: Spring, summer, fall.
COMMENTS: Three species of *Eupatorium*
are reported to occur on the barrier
islands. *E. compositifolium* has erect stems,
the leaves or leaf segments are very
narrow, and the flowers are white.
E. azureum has erect stems and the leaves
are up to 1½" broad. *E. betonicifolium* has
weak, sprawling stems.

   Also known as *Tamaulipa azurea*.

Mist Flower

FAMILY: Compositae
SCIENTIFIC NAME: *Eupatorium betonicifolium*
STEMS: Somewhat woody, weak and falling over, rooting at the nodes.
LEAVES: Opposite. Blades succulent, mostly oblong, up to 1¾" long and ¾" broad. The margins are toothed.
FLOWERS: In heads about ⁵⁄₁₆" tall. There are no ray flowers. All flowers are disk-type, bluish in color.
FRUIT: Achenes about ¹⁄₁₆" tall with pappus bristles ⅛" long.
HABITAT: Sand or sandy clay, throughout the Texas coast.
BLOOM PERIOD: Spring, summer.
COMMENTS: Also known as *Conoclinium betonicifolium*. The three species of *Eupatorium* are compared above.

Rabbit Tobacco

FAMILY: Compositae
SCIENTIFIC NAME: *Evax verna*
STEMS: All over gray woolly, to 6" tall.
LEAVES: Alternate, gray woolly. Blades mostly spatulate, up to ¾" long.
FLOWERS: In small heads almost completely hidden by the woolly hairs. Ray flowers absent. Disk flowers minute.
FRUIT: Achenes less than ¹⁄₁₆" long, without pappus.
HABITAT: Sandy clay, Padre and Mustang Islands.
BLOOM PERIOD: Spring.
COMMENTS: This plant is best recognized by its covering of gray woolly hairs. The flower heads would likely go unnoticed because of this covering.

Flaveria

FAMILY: Compositae
SCIENTIFIC NAME: *Flaveria brownii*
STEMS: Erect, up to 28" tall.
LEAVES: Opposite. Blades linear, up to 4¾" long and ¼" broad.
FLOWERS: In heads about ⅛" broad. Ray flowers absent. Disk flowers yellow, about ¹⁄₁₆" long.
FRUIT: Achenes about ¹⁄₁₆" long, without pappus.
HABITAT: Sandy areas, throughout the Texas coast.
BLOOM PERIOD: Summer, fall.
COMMENTS: Also known as *Flaveria oppositifolia*.

Florestina

FAMILY: Compositae
SCIENTIFIC NAME: *Florestina tripteris*
STEMS: Erect, up to 24" tall.
LEAVES: Lower leaves opposite, the upper ones alternate and compound with 3 leaflets. The leaflets grow up to 2⅛" long.
FLOWERS: In heads about ¼" tall. Ray flowers absent. Disk flowers white.
FRUIT: Achenes about ⅛" tall, with pappus of tiny scales.
HABITAT: Sandy clay, Padre Island.
BLOOM PERIOD: Spring, summer, fall.

Indian Blanket, Firewheel

FAMILY: Compositae
SCIENTIFIC NAME: *Gaillardia pulchella*
STEMS: Erect, up to 24" tall.
LEAVES: Alternate. Blades more or less lanceolate, up to 5" long and 1" broad. Margins on the larger leaves are lobed. Leaves higher on the stem are much smaller.
FLOWERS: In heads about 1¾" broad. Ray flowers red, tipped with yellow, varying from almost all red to almost all yellow, about ⅝" long. Disk flowers purplish red.
FRUIT: Achenes about 1/16" tall with pappus of scales about 3/16" long.
HABITAT: Widespread, in sandy soil throughout the Texas coast.
BLOOM PERIOD: Spring, summer.
COMMENTS: Indian Blankets are seen growing singly or in large groups. They are among our most attractive wildflowers and are sometimes cultivated.

Cudweed

FAMILY: Compositae
SCIENTIFIC NAME: *Gnaphalium pensilvanicum*
STEMS: Erect, gray woolly, up to 16" tall.
LEAVES: Alternate, gray woolly, the blades oblanceolate, up to 2¾" long and ¾" broad.
FLOWERS: In heads mostly hidden by the woolly hairs. Ray flowers absent. Disk flowers inconspicuous.
FRUIT: Achenes less than ¹⁄₁₆" tall. Pappus bristles about ⅛" long.
HABITAT: Sandy soils, Padre and Matagorda Islands.
BLOOM PERIOD: Spring.
COMMENTS: There are similarities of this species with *Evax,* but the achenes of *Evax* have no pappus, and its leaves are smaller.

Also known as *Gamochaeta pensilvanica.*

Sneezeweed

FAMILY: Compositae
SCIENTIFIC NAME: *Helenium amarum*
STEMS: Erect, up to 20" or taller.
LEAVES: Alternate, mostly linear and threadlike, malodorous when crushed.
FLOWERS: In heads up to 1" broad. Ray flowers yellow, about ⁵⁄₁₆" long. Disk flowers yellow, on a hemisphere-shaped receptacle.
FRUIT: Achenes less than ¹⁄₁₆" tall, with tiny pappus scales.
HABITAT: Sandy clay, Padre and Matagorda Islands.
BLOOM PERIOD: Summer, fall.
COMMENTS: Sneezeweed is easily recognized by its threadlike leaves and its disk flowers arranged in a hemispherical shape.

Photographed at Lady Bird Johnson Wildflower Center, Austin, Texas

Common Sunflower

FAMILY: Compositae

SCIENTIFIC NAME: *Helianthus annuus*

STEMS: Erect, with stiff hairs, often growing over 6' tall.

LEAVES: Opposite on lower parts, alternate higher up. Petioles up to 4¼" long. Blades ovate to triangular, up to 6" long and 6" broad.

FLOWERS: In heads up to 4" broad. Ray flowers yellow, about 1⅛" long. Disk flowers purplish brown.

FRUIT: Achenes up to ³⁄₁₆" tall. Pappus consists of 2 pointed scales less than ¹⁄₁₆" long.

HABITAT: Sandy clay, Padre and Matagorda Islands.

BLOOM PERIOD: Spring, summer, fall.

COMMENTS: Two other species of *Helianthus* occur on the barrier islands. They are easily distinguished. *H. argophyllus* grows as tall as or taller than *H. annuus,* but its leaves are all silver-colored. *H. praecox* subsp. *runyonii* grows only 24" tall. It can be distinguished from short forms of *H. annuus* by examining the outer phyllaries. In *H. annuus,* they are abruptly pointed; in *H. praecox* subsp. *runyonii,* they taper gradually to a point.

Silverleaf Sunflower

FAMILY: Compositae

SCIENTIFIC NAME: *Helianthus argophyllus*

STEMS: Erect, up to 12' or taller.

LEAVES: Mostly alternate and ovate, up to 12" long, covered with soft white hairs that give a silvery appearance.

FLOWERS: In heads up to 4" broad. Ray flowers yellow, disk flowers brown.

FRUIT: Achenes up to ³⁄₁₆" tall. Pappus consists of 2 pointed scales about ¹⁄₁₆" long.

HABITAT: Sandy soil, Padre, Mustang, and Matagorda Islands.

BLOOM PERIOD: Summer, fall.

COMMENTS: See *H. annuus* for distinguishing characteristics.

Sunflower

FAMILY: Compositae
SCIENTIFIC NAME: *Helianthus praecox*
subsp. *runyonii*
STEMS: Erect, to about 24" tall, rough to
the touch.
LEAVES: Mostly alternate. Petioles up to
1½" long. Blades ovate to triangular, up to
2⅛" long and 1⅛" broad.
FLOWERS: In heads about 2¼" broad. Ray
flowers yellow, about ¾" long. Disk
flowers brown.
FRUIT: Achenes about ⅛" tall. Pappus
consists of 2 tiny pointed scales.
HABITAT: Sandy clay, loose sand, Padre,
Matagorda, and Galveston Islands.
BLOOM PERIOD: Spring, summer, fall.
COMMENTS: See *H. annuus* for
distinguishing characteristics.

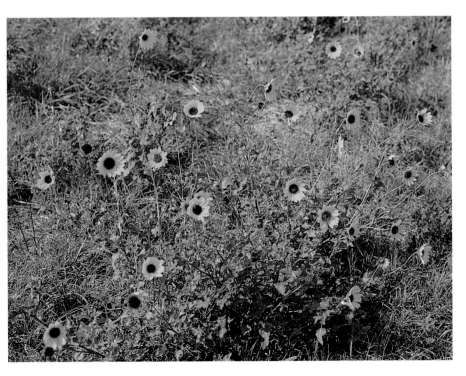

Camphor Weed

FAMILY: Compositae
SCIENTIFIC NAME: *Heterotheca subaxillaris*
STEMS: Erect, up to 39" tall.
LEAVES: Alternate. Blades mostly oblong to obovate, up to 2⅜" long and 1" broad, the margins mostly smooth.
FLOWERS: In heads up to 1⅛" broad. Ray flowers yellow, about ¼" long. Disk flowers yellow.
FRUIT: Achenes ⅛" tall or less. Those from the ray flowers are without pappus. Those from the disk flowers have a pappus up to ³⁄₁₆" long.
HABITAT: Growing in sand, throughout the Texas beaches.
BLOOM PERIOD: Spring, fall.
COMMENTS: The plants produce a camphor odor when bruised. The Camphor Daisy (*Machaeranthera phyllocephala*) also has a camphor odor, but its leaves have prominent teeth.

Woolly White

FAMILY: Compositae
SCIENTIFIC NAME: *Hymenopappus artemisiifolius*
STEMS: Biennials up to 3' tall, usually less.
LEAVES: Whitish, especially on the lower surfaces. Blades up to 8" long with margins that vary from nearly smooth to deeply cut.
FLOWERS: In heads up to ½" broad. Ray flowers absent, disk flowers white.
FRUIT: Achenes about ⅛" long, 4-sided, with a pappus of 8 or 9 scales ⅛" long or less.
HABITAT: Sandy soils, Goose Island.
BLOOM PERIOD: Spring, summer.

Sumpweed

FAMILY: Compositae
SCIENTIFIC NAME: *Iva angustifolia*
STEMS: Erect, up to 39" or taller.
LEAVES: Opposite on lower stems, alternate higher up. Blades lanceolate to linear, up to 1½" long and ¼" broad.
FLOWERS: Tiny, crowded in small heads ³⁄₁₆" tall, hanging downward. Separate male and female flowers are located in the same head.
FRUIT: Achenes about ¹⁄₁₆" tall, without pappus.
HABITAT: Sand, throughout the Texas beaches.
BLOOM PERIOD: Summer, fall.
COMMENTS: This species resembles *Ambrosia psilostachya.* In *A. psilostachya,* male and female flowers are in separate heads, and the female involucres are spiny. In *Iva angustifolia,* male and female flowers are in the same head, and the involucres are not spiny. The large bushy growth habit of *I. frutescens* distinguishes it from the other related species.

Shrubby Sumpweed

FAMILY: Compositae
SCIENTIFIC NAME: *Iva frutescens*
STEMS: Erect, bushy, up to 6' tall or more.
LEAVES: Lanceolate, with toothed margins, up to 3½" long.
FLOWERS: Tiny, in small heads hanging downward.
FRUIT: Achenes brown, up to ⅛" long, with tiny dots of resin. Pappus absent.
HABITAT: Sandy soil, throughout most of the Texas coast.
BLOOM PERIOD: Summer, fall.
COMMENTS: This species is easy to distinguish by its robust, bushy growth.

Camphor Daisy

FAMILY: Compositae

SCIENTIFIC NAME: *Machaeranthera phyllocephala*

STEMS: Erect, up to 24" or taller.

LEAVES: Alternate, without petioles. Blades mostly oblanceolate, up to 2" long and ⅝" broad. Margins sharp-toothed or lobed.

FLOWERS: In heads up to 1½" broad. Ray flowers yellow, about ⅜" long. Disk flowers yellow.

FRUIT: Achenes about 1/16" tall with pappus bristles ¼" long.

HABITAT: Sandy soil, throughout the Texas beaches.

BLOOM PERIOD: Spring, summer, fall.

COMMENTS: When bruised, the plants exude a camphor odor. They are distinguished from Camphor Weed by the leaf margins, which are sharp-toothed or lobed.

Climbing Hempweed

FAMILY: Compositae
SCIENTIFIC NAME: *Mikania scandens*
STEMS: Perennial twining vines.
LEAVES: Opposite, the blades triangular to heart-shaped, up to 3⅛" long.
FLOWERS: In heads about ¼" tall. Ray flowers absent. Disk flowers white.
FRUIT: Achenes less than ⅛" tall, with pappus of bristles about ³⁄₁₆" long.
HABITAT: Usually moist soils, Galveston Island.
BLOOM PERIOD: Summer, fall.

Palafoxia

FAMILY: Compositae
SCIENTIFIC NAME: *Palafoxia texana* var.
ambigua
STEMS: Erect, up to 39" or taller.
LEAVES: Alternate. Blades lanceolate, up to
3⅛" long and ½" broad.
FLOWERS: In heads ½" to ⅝" tall. Ray
flowers absent. Disk flowers lavender to
purple, with blackish-purple anthers.
FRUIT: Achenes about ¼" tall with pappus
of scales ⅛" tall or less.
HABITAT: Sandy soil, throughout the Texas
beaches.
BLOOM PERIOD: Spring, summer, fall.
COMMENTS: This plant is quite variable as
to size of leaves and flowers. Some plants
may be little more than 12" tall.

P. *rosea* grows on Padre Island. Its leaves
are less than ¼" broad, narrower than
those of P. *texana*. P. *hookeriana* also grows
on Padre Island. The ray florets in its
heads distinguish it from the other two
species.

False Ragweed

FAMILY: Compositae
SCIENTIFIC NAME: *Parthenium hysterophorus*
STEMS: Erect, up to 39" tall, highly branched.
LEAVES: Alternate. Blades up to 8" long and 3" broad, becoming much smaller up the stem. Margins usually lobed twice unless the leaves are very small. Then the margins are not lobed.
FLOWERS: In numerous small heads about ³⁄₁₆" broad, resembling tiny heads of cauliflower. There are 5 tiny white ray flowers less than ¹⁄₁₆" long. The disk flowers are white, on a convex receptacle.
FRUIT: Achenes are flattened, about ¹⁄₁₆" tall with pappus of 2 pointed scales. They are produced only by the ray flowers.
HABITAT: Sandy clay, Padre Island.
BLOOM PERIOD: Spring, summer, fall.
COMMENTS: Although recorded only on Padre Island, False Ragweed is probably more widespread.

Stinkweed

FAMILY: Compositae
SCIENTIFIC NAME: *Pluchea odorata*
STEMS: Erect, growing to almost 5' tall.
LEAVES: Alternate. Blades ovate, up to 6"
long and 2¾" broad.
FLOWERS: In numerous heads about ¼"
tall. Ray flowers absent. Disk flowers and
phyllaries purple.
FRUIT: Achenes less than ¹⁄₁₆" tall with
pappus of bristles about ⅛" long.
HABITAT: Moist places, throughout the
Texas coast.
BLOOM PERIOD: Summer, fall.
COMMENTS: Also known as *Pluchea
purpurascens.*

False Dandelion

FAMILY: Compositae
SCIENTIFIC NAME: *Pyrrhopappus pauciflorus*
STEMS: At first very short, hidden by the
leaves. Later, with the flower stalk, it
grows up to 22" tall.
LEAVES: Crowded toward the base. Blades
usually lobed, up to 6" long and 1¼"
broad. Leaves and all other parts of the
plant bleed milky sap when broken.
FLOWERS: In solitary heads up to 1⅜"
broad. Flowers are all yellow, similar to the
more common ray flowers, but with 5
lobes instead of 3.
FRUIT: Achenes almost ¼" tall, topped by
a threadlike beak. Pappus bristles up to
⁵⁄₁₆" long.
HABITAT: Sandy clay, Padre Island.
BLOOM PERIOD: Spring.
COMMENTS: The true dandelion does not
grow in this area. It produces an
inflorescence with only 1 head of flowers.
The false dandelion produces a branching
inflorescence with several heads.

Mexican Hat

FAMILY: Compositae
SCIENTIFIC NAME: *Ratibida columnaris*
STEMS: Erect, up to 4' tall, usually shorter.
LEAVES: Opposite on the lower stems, alternate higher up. Blades once- or twice-lobed, up to 5½" long and 2⅜" broad.
FLOWERS: In heads on long stalks. Ray flowers variable in color from yellow throughout with a red-brown basal spot, to red-brown throughout. Disk flowers are on a tall cylindrical receptacle and are brownish in color.
FRUIT: Achenes are about ¹⁄₁₆" tall, with a microscopic pappus.
HABITAT: Sandy clay, Padre and Matagorda Islands.

BLOOM PERIOD: Spring, summer, fall.
COMMENTS: This species is very commonly seen inland. It is quite similar to *Ratibida peduncularis,* which is more abundant at the coast.

Also known as *Ratibida columnifera.*

Mexican Hat

FAMILY: Compositae
SCIENTIFIC NAME: *Ratibida peduncularis*
STEMS: Erect, up to 3' tall, usually shorter.
LEAVES: Mostly crowded at the base, opposite on lower stems, alternate higher up. Those higher on the stem are noticeably smaller. Blades once- or twice-lobed, up to 5½" long and 2⅜" broad.
FLOWERS: In heads on long stalks. Ray flowers variable in color, from yellow with a basal red-brown spot, to almost all red-brown. Disk flowers reddish-brown, on a tall cylindrical receptacle.
FRUIT: Achenes about 3/16" tall, with a microscopic pappus.
HABITAT: Sandy clay, Boca Chica Beach; Brazos, Padre, Mustang, and Matagorda Islands.
BLOOM PERIOD: Spring, summer, fall.
COMMENTS: This species and *Ratibida columnaris* can be easily confused. In *R. columnaris,* the leaves are all more or less the same size, whereas in *R. peduncularis* the upper leaves are usually smaller than the lower ones. Also, the achenes on *R. columnaris* are smaller than those of *R. peduncularis.*

Cone Flower

FAMILY: Compositae
SCIENTIFIC NAME: *Rudbeckia hirta* var. *angustifolia*
STEMS: Erect, up to 24" tall.
LEAVES: Mostly alternate. Blades ovate, up to 6" long and 1⅜" broad.
FLOWERS: In solitary heads up to 2" broad. Ray flowers yellow with reddish-brown basal spots. Disk flowers reddish-brown, on a conical receptacle.
FRUIT: Achenes less than ¹⁄₁₆" tall, without pappus, or sometimes with a pappus of 2 to 4 tiny teeth.
HABITAT: Sandy soil, Padre, Mustang, Matagorda, and Galveston Islands.
BLOOM PERIOD: Spring, summer.
COMMENTS: At a glance, these flowers might resemble those of *Ratibida,* but Cone Flower has a broader, cone-shaped (not cylindrical) receptacle.

Groundsel

FAMILY: Compositae
SCIENTIFIC NAME: *Senecio ampullaceus*
STEMS: Erect, up to 32" tall.
LEAVES: Alternate. Blades obovate, up to 6" long and 1½" broad. Margins on the upper leaves often toothed.
FLOWERS: In heads up to 1⅛" broad. Ray flowers yellow, about ⁵⁄₁₆" long. Disk flowers yellow.
FRUIT: Achenes less than ⅛" tall, with pappus bristles about ³⁄₁₆" long.
HABITAT: Sandy soil, Padre Island.
BLOOM PERIOD: Spring.
COMMENTS: The generic name, *Senecio,* is sometimes confused with Cenizo, the common name for *Leucophyllum frutescens,* sometimes called sage.

Some plants with flowers, others with white seed heads

Ragwort

FAMILY: Compositae
SCIENTIFIC NAME: *Senecio riddellii*
STEMS: Erect, up to 39" tall.
LEAVES: Alternate and succulent. Blades a blue-gray color, about 2¾" long and 1½" broad. Margins greatly dissected, the lobes linear.
FLOWERS: In heads about 1⅛" broad. Ray flowers yellow, about ⁵⁄₁₆" long. Disk flowers yellow.
FRUIT: Achenes up to ⅛" tall, with pappus bristles about ¼" long.
HABITAT: Sandy soil, Brazos, Padre, Mustang, and Matagorda Islands.
BLOOM PERIOD: Mostly fall. Some spring.
COMMENTS: This species is easily distinguished from *S. ampullaceus* by its blue-green leaves with linear lobes.

Tall Goldenrod

FAMILY: Compositae
SCIENTIFIC NAME: *Solidago canadensis*
STEMS: Erect, 5½' tall or more.
LEAVES: Alternate, the blades narrow, about 2¾" long and ⅜" broad.
FLOWERS: Heads about ¼" tall, very crowded on one side of the flowering branches, the branch tips curling. Ray flowers and disk flowers yellow.
FRUIT: Achenes very tiny with bristles less than ⅛" tall.
HABITAT: Various soils, Galveston Island.
BLOOM PERIOD: Fall.
COMMENTS: *S. canadensis* is distinguished from *S. sempervirens* by its many short hairs. *S. sempervirens* is not hairy. *S. canadensis* has also been known as *S. altissima*.

Seaside Goldenrod

FAMILY: Compositae
SCIENTIFIC NAME: *Solidago sempervirens* var. *mexicana*
STEMS: Erect, growing up to 6' tall, usually shorter.
LEAVES: Alternate, blades linear or elliptic, up to 7" long and ⅝" broad.
FLOWERS: In crowded small heads, the branch tips curling. Heads about ⁵⁄₁₆" tall. Ray flowers yellow, not noticeable. Disk flowers yellow.
FRUIT: Achenes less than ¹⁄₁₆" tall, with pappus bristles about ⅛" long.
HABITAT: Sandy soils, Brazos, Padre, and Matagorda Islands.
BLOOM PERIOD: Summer, fall.
COMMENTS: Seaside goldenrod is quickly recognized by its cluster of yellow heads in coils. Its lack of hairs distinguishes it from *S. canadensis.*

Common Sow Thistle

FAMILY: Compositae

SCIENTIFIC NAME: *Sonchus oleraceus*

STEMS: Erect, growing up to 39" or taller.

LEAVES: Alternate. Blades up to 6" long and 3½" broad, lobed and sharp-toothed, with a pair of basal "ears." When broken, all parts of the plant bleed milky sap.

FLOWERS: In heads about 1" broad. Flowers yellow, similar to ray flowers but with 5 lobes.

FRUIT: Achenes up to ⅛" tall with pappus bristles ¼" long.

HABITAT: Various soils, throughout the Texas coast.

BLOOM PERIOD: Mostly spring, but can bloom all seasons.

COMMENTS: A second species, *S. asper,* grows to a lesser extent on the barrier islands. The two species are distinguished by the shape of the "ears" at the bases of the leaves. In *S. asper,* they are toothed but rounded in outline. In *S. oleraceus,* they are toothed and taper to an acute angle.

Showy Nerveray

FAMILY: Compositae
SCIENTIFIC NAME: *Tetragonotheca repanda*
STEMS: Erect, up to 24" tall.
LEAVES: Opposite. Blades mostly ovate or triangular, up to 4¼" long.
FLOWERS: Heads solitary, up to 2½" broad. Ray flowers yellow, disk flowers yellow. Involucre consists of 4 phyllaries.
FRUIT: Achenes 4-sided, about ⅛" tall. Pappus tiny or absent.
HABITAT: Sandy soils, Padre and Mustang Islands.
BLOOM PERIOD: Summer, fall.
COMMENTS: This member of the Compositae family is easy to identify because of its involucre made of 4 phyllaries.

Green Thread

FAMILY: Compositae
SCIENTIFIC NAME: *Thelesperma filifolium*
STEMS: Erect, up to 20" tall.
LEAVES: Opposite, the blades dissected
and the segments narrow and threadlike.
FLOWERS: Heads solitary, about 1½"
broad. Ray flowers yellow. Disk flowers
purplish-brown.
FRUIT: Achenes various shapes, up to ¼"
long, usually less. Pappus of 2 triangular
awns.
HABITAT: Sandy soils, Padre, Mustang, and
Matagorda Islands.
BLOOM PERIOD: Spring, summer.
COMMENTS: *T. filifolium* and *T. nuecense* are
similar in appearance. The ray flowers of
T. filifolium are solid yellow, while those of
T. nuecense have at least some reddish-
brown color, sometimes only at the base.

Green Thread

FAMILY: Compositae
SCIENTIFIC NAME: *Thelesperma nuecense*
STEMS: Erect, up to 39" tall.
LEAVES: Opposite, the blades dissected
and the segments narrow and threadlike.
FLOWERS: Heads solitary, up to 2⅛"
broad. Ray flowers golden yellow with
reddish-brown coloring toward the base
(sometimes almost all reddish-brown).
Disk flowers purplish-brown.
FRUIT: Achenes about ¼" tall, with
pappus of 2 tiny triangular awns.
HABITAT: Sandy soils, Padre Island.
BLOOM PERIOD: Spring.
COMMENTS: *T. nuecense* is not as
widespread on the coast as *T. filifolium*.

Tiny Tim

FAMILY: Compositae
SCIENTIFIC NAME: *Thymophylla tenuiloba*
STEMS: Short and branched, up to 8" tall, the plants rounded.
LEAVES: Alternate, the blades highly dissected and the segments threadlike.
FLOWERS: Heads solitary, ½"–1" broad. Ray flowers yellow, disk flowers yellow.
FRUIT: Achenes about ⅛" tall. The pappus is of scales about ⅛" tall.
HABITAT: Roadsides, sandy soils, Boca Chica Beach, Brazos and Padre Islands.
BLOOM PERIOD: Spring, summer, fall.
COMMENTS: Also called *Dyssodia tenuiloba*.

T. pentachaeta grows on Padre Island. The two species are very similar and sometimes difficult to distinguish.

Cowpen Daisy

FAMILY: Compositae
SCIENTIFIC NAME: *Verbesina encelioides*
STEMS: Erect, up to 3' tall.
LEAVES: Mostly opposite, the blades
triangular, up to 4¼" long.
FLOWERS: In heads up to 2" broad. Disk
flowers yellow, ray flowers yellow.
FRUIT: Achenes flattened, often with small
"wings," up to ¼" tall. Pappus of tiny
awns.
HABITAT: Sandy soils, Padre, Mustang, and
Matagorda Islands.
BLOOM PERIOD: Spring and fall.
COMMENTS: This is among our more
showy and attractive wildflowers.

Cocklebur

FAMILY: Compositae
SCIENTIFIC NAME: *Xanthium strumarium*
STEMS: Erect, up to 6' tall or more.
LEAVES: Mostly alternate. Blades usually
more or less 3-lobed and heart-shaped
basally, up to 4¾" long and 4" broad.
FLOWERS: Very tiny and inconspicuous, in
spiny heads.
FRUIT: Achenes are inconspicuous, hidden
inside the spiny heads.
HABITAT: Various soils, throughout the
barrier islands.
BLOOM PERIOD: Summer, fall.
COMMENTS: The spiny heads (cockleburs)
are the distinguishing feature of this
species.

Glossary

Achene. A small, dry, indehiscent, 1-seeded fruit, typical of the Compositae and Cyperaceae families.

Alternate. Leaves occurring singly at a given point on a stem.

Annual. A plant that produces flowers and fruit in one season and then dies.

Anther. The part of the stamen that produces pollen.

Awn. A very small bristle.

Axil. The angle formed where the leaf petiole joins the stem.

Axillary. Originating at the angle formed where the leaf petiole joins the stem.

Berry. A juicy, many-seeded fruit.

Biennial. A plant that produces flowers and fruit in its second season and then dies.

Bilateral. One, and only one, line through the center will divide the flower into 2 mirror images. Example: an orchid flower.

Bract. A modification of a leaf, found associated with some inflorescences.

Calyx. The sepals of a flower, collectively.

Capsule. A dry fruit made of more than 1 carpel and that usually breaks open.

Carpel. The unit that makes up a pistil; there may be 1 or more.

Catkin. An inflorescence composed of many small, unisexual flowers that lack petals.

Compound leaf. A leaf divided into 2 or more leaflets.

Cordate. Heart-shaped.

Corolla. The petals of the flower, collectively.

Dehiscent. Breaking open.

Disk flower. In the Compositae, radially symmetrical flowers that emerge from the disk, or central portion.

Drupe. A juicy, 1-seeded fruit, the seed enclosed in a hard covering—a peach, for example.

Elliptic. A flat figure broadest at or about the middle and tapering to both ends.

Entire. Smooth.

Filament. The lower part of the stamen, usually threadlike.

Floret. A very small flower, one of a cluster, as in the Compositae and Gramineae families.

Fruit. A matured ovary. The structure with the enclosed seeds.

Head. A cluster of flowers attached to a common receptacle.

Indehiscent. Characteristic of a fruit that does not split open.

Inferior ovary. The sepals and petals are attached to the side or the top of the ovary.

Inflorescence. The flowering stalk.

Infructescence. The fruiting stalk.

Involucre. A cluster of bracts below a flower cluster, especially in the Compositae family.

Lanceolate. Lance-shaped. Narrowly ovate.

Leaf blade. The broad, flattened part of the leaf.

Leaf margin. The edge of a leaf blade.

Leaf petiole. The narrow stalk that connects the leaf blade with the stem. It is not always present.

Legume. A fruit consisting of a single carpel, breaking open along 2 sides—a string bean, for example. Also used to refer to a member of the Leguminosae family.

Linear. Long and narrow, the sides more or less parallel.

Node. (1) The point on a stem where a leaf emerges. (2) A swollen place.

Nutlet. Occurs in a dry fruit that separates into several (usually 4) small, 1-seeded, nutlike segments. Especially found in families Verbenaceae, Labiatae, and Boraginaceae.

Obcordate. Heart-shaped, but the heart is upside down.

Oblanceolate. The reverse of lanceolate. The point of the lance is attached to the leaf petiole.

Oblong. The length is greater than the width, and the sides are more or less parallel.

Obovate. Broadest toward the apex, narrowing toward the base. See *ovate.*

Once compound. The simple division of a leaf blade into leaflets to form a compound leaf.

Opposite. Two leaves (or branches or flowers) originating at the same height (node) on the stem (or axis), but on opposite sides.

Ovary. The swollen part of the pistil that encloses the ovules. After pollination and fertilization, the ovary grows to become the fruit with the seeds (the matured ovules) inside.

Ovate. A flat figure, broader below the middle (toward the petiole), tapering toward the apex.

Palmate venation. The major veins of a leaf originate from the same point at the base.

Palmately compound. The leaflets of a compound leaf all arise from a common point.

Pappus. In the Compositae family, a modification of the calyx that can have various forms. It is most noticeable as the "parachute" attached to the dandelion fruit.

Pedicel. The individual stalk of a single flower.

Peduncle. The main supporting stalk of the whole inflorescence.

Perennial. Lives year after year, producing flowers and fruit.

Perfect. A flower that has both male (stamens) and female (pistil) parts.

Petal. One of the second set of appendages of a flower, usually the showy part. Example, the colorful part of a rose flower.

Phyllary. One of a cluster of bracts (the involucre) that appears below a cluster of flowers, as in the Compositae family.

Pistil. The female part of a flower, consisting of the stigma, style, and ovary.

Prickle. Sharp outgrowths of the bark, as on a rosebush.

Raceme. An unbranched inflorescence, each flower having a pedicel attaching it to the main flower stalk, or axis.

Rachis. In a compound leaf, the portion of the axis to which the leaflets are attached.

Radial. Refers to the outline of a flower. Any of several lines drawn through the center will divide the flower into two equal halves or mirror images. See *bilateral.*

Ray flower. In the Compositae family, a bilateral, straplike flower occurring around the edge of the disk.

Receptacle. The enlarged end of the stem to which the floral parts are attached.

Rhizome. An underground, more or less horizontal stem.

Rosette. A crowded cluster of leaves at the base of a plant.

Sepal. One of the lowest whorl of appendages of a flower, sometimes green (as in roses), or sometimes colored (as in lilies and orchids).

Simple leaf. A leaf that is not compound.

Spatulate. In the shape of a knife rounded on the end, and tapering toward the base.

Spike. An unbranched inflorescence in which the flowers are attached directly to the axis (main flowering stalk), without pedicels.

Spikelets. In a compound inflorescence, a secondary spike of flowers, especially in the Cyperaceae family.

Spur. A tubelike projection from the base of a flower corolla. It usually contains nectar.

Stamen. The male part of a flower, consisting of filament and anther. The anther produces the pollen.

Stigma. The sticky portion at the top of the pistil of a flower. Pollen will adhere to this part.

Stipule. A small appendage at the base of some leaves. They occur in pairs.

Style. The narrow part of the pistil, between the stigma and the ovary.

Succulent. Thickened and juicy.

Superior ovary. The sepals, petals, etc., are attached at the base of the ovary.

Synonym. Another name a plant was given, incorrectly applied and not valid.

Tendril. In vines, a wiry appendage coming from a stem or leaf and wrapping itself around a support.

Toothed. With small indentations in the leaf margin.

Transverse. Across the width.

Triangular. In the shape of a triangle.

Twice compound. The primary segments of a compound leaf (pinnae) are further divided into smaller segments (leaflets).

Twining. A stem of a vine that climbs by winding itself around a support.

Umbel. An umbrella-shaped inflorescence in which all the pedicels are attached to a common point.

Unisexual. Of 1 sex, as in plants that have separate male and female flowers.

Whorled. Three or more leaves (or sometimes other parts) arising in a circle around the stem at the same height.

Bibliography

Britton, J. C., and B. Morton. 1989. *Shore Ecology of the Gulf of Mexico.* University of Texas Press. 387 pp.

Cannatella, Mary M., and Rita Arnold. 1958. *Plants of the Texas Shore.* Texas A&M University Press. 77 pp.

Cheatham, Scooter, and M. C. Johnston, with L. Marshall. 1995. *The Useful Wild Plants of Texas, the Southeastern and Southwestern United States, the Southern Plains, and Northern Mexico,* vol. 1. Useful Wild Plants, Inc. 568 pp.

Correll, D. S., and M. C. Johnston. 1970. *Manual of the Vascular Plants of Texas.* Texas Research Foundation. 1881 pp.

Gillespie, T. S. 1976. "The Flowering Plants of Mustang Island, Texas— An Annotated Checklist." *Texas Journal of Science* 27: 131–148.

Hartman, R. L., and J. Smith. 1973. "A Floristic and Ecological Study of Matagorda Island." In *Matagorda Island: A Natural Area Survey.* LBJ School of Public Affairs, University of Texas at Austin, pp. 116–145.

Hatch, S. L., et al. 1999. *Grasses of the Texas Gulf Prairies and Marshes.* Texas A&M University Press.

Johnston, M. C. 1990. *The Vascular Plants of Texas: A List, Up-dating the Manual of the Vascular Plants of Texas,* Second Edition. Marshall C. Johnston. 107 pp.

Jones, Fred B. 1975. *Flora of the Texas Coastal Bend.* Mission Press. 262 pp.

Jones, Stanley D., Joseph K. Wipff, and Paul M. Montgomery. 1997. *Vascular Plants of Texas.* University of Texas Press. 404 pp.

Lonard, R. I. 1993. *Guide to the Grasses of the Lower Rio Grande Valley, Texas.* University of Texas–Pan American Press. 240 pp.

Lonard, R. I., and F. W. Judd. 1980. "Phytogeography of South Padre Island, Texas." *Southwestern Naturalist* 25 (3): 313–322.

Lonard, R. I., Frank W. Judd, and Sammie L. Sides. 1978. "Annotated Checklist of the Flowering Plants of South Padre Island, Texas." *Southwestern Naturalist* 23 (3): 497–510.

McAlister, Wayne H., and Martha K. McAlister. 1995. *Aransas: A Naturalist's Guide.* University of Texas Press. 392 pp.

McAlister, Wayne H., and Martha K. McAlister. 1993. *Matagorda Island: A Naturalist's Guide.* University of Texas Press. 354 pp.

Negrete, I. G., et al. 1999. "A Checklist for the Vascular Plants of Padre Island National Seashore." *Sida Contributions to Botany* vol. 18, no. 4. 1227–1245.

Richardson, Alfred T. 1995. *Plants of the Rio Grande Delta.* University of Texas Press. 332 pp.

Stutzenbaker, Charles D. 1999. *Aquatic and Wetland Plants of the Western Gulf Coast.* University of Texas Press. 465 pp.

Sullivan, J. Rodney, and Alfred Richardson. "Survey of the Plants of Brazos Island State Park." In manuscript.

Texas Parks and Wildlife. 1989. "Preliminary Checklist of Vascular Plants of Galveston Island State Park, Galveston County, Texas." Unpublished.

Texas Parks and Wildlife. 1996. "Preliminary Checklist of Vascular Plants of Goose Island State Recreation Area, Aransas County, Texas." Unpublished.

Texas Parks and Wildlife. 1989. "Preliminary Checklist of Vascular Plants of Mustang Island State Park, Nueces County, Texas." Unpublished.

Index